The Hulton Getty Picture Collection & Allsport *Decades of Sport*

Horse Racing

Pferderennen
Courses hippiques

D0381423

The Hulton Getty Picture Collection & Allsport *Decades of Sport*

Horse Racing
Pferderennen
Courses hippiques

Jamie Douglas-Home

KÖNEMANN

First published in 2000 by Könemann Verlagsgesellschaft mbH, Bonner Straße 126, D-50968 Köln

This book was produced by The Hulton Getty Picture Collection Limited,
Unique House, 21–31 Woodfield Road, London W9 2BA

For Könemann:	For Hulton Getty:
Managing editor: Sally Bald	Art direction: Alex Linghorn
Project editors: Sabine Gerber,	Design & production: Tea McAleer
Robert von Radetzky	Editor: Richard Collins
German translation: Oliver Fröschke	Proof reader & indexer: Liz Ihre
French translation: Denis Sartor	Special thanks: Rob Harbourne,
Production: Alexandra Kiesling, Nicola Leurs	Karen Leach, Mary Welland, Antonia Hille

Typesetting by argus Korrekturservice, Cologne. Colour separation by Omniascanners Srl., Milan
Printed and bound by Star Standard Industries Ltd., Singapore
Printed in Singapore

ISBN 3-8290-3624-8
10 9 8 7 6 5 4 3 2 1

Frontispiece: Glassy-eyed punter. Armed with the essential tools of the
trade, an elegantly attired racegoer keeps an eagle eye on proceedings
at the Epsom Derby, June 1923.

Frontispiz: Spieler mit Glasaugen. Ausgestattet mit dem wichtigsten
Werkzeug, hat dieser elegant gekleidete Rennzuschauer ein Adlerauge
auf die Ereignisse beim Epsom Derby, Juni 1923.

Frontispiece : Un parieur aux yeux de verre. Equipé de l'instrument
de base, ce spectateur élégant observe comme un aigle les événements
lors du Derby d'Epsom en juin 1923.

Contents/Inhalt/Sommaire

Introduction

Although horse racing still clings resolutely to tradition, there have been great sea-changes in the sport in the 20th century. Top hats and tails for men are still the dress code in the Royal Enclosure at Royal Ascot, as in King Edward VII's day. Jockeys' silks, breeches and boots look much as they have always done. But, unlike human athletes, horses do not go much faster now than they did a hundred years ago. Bloodstock values have soared; today a top-class thoroughbred is a very valuable commodity indeed. World-wide, racing has ceased to be merely a sport: it is now big business. The Sport of Kings has become the sport of desert princes. Oil-rich Arab sheikhs have begun the new millennium as the most prominent owners on the international racing stage.

In the 20th century, racing had its fair share of equine champions and heroes, among them Red Rum, triple Grand National winner; Ribot, Italian champion of the 1950s; Sea Bird II, the classiest Derby winner of all; and Secretariat, the US Triple Crown victor of the 1970s, all won the hearts of an adoring public. The tragic losers, too, played their part: the Queen Mother's steeplechaser, Devon Loch, who inexplicably fell on the flat with the 1956 Grand National at his mercy; the Derby winner, Shergar, kidnapped and so cruelly destroyed in his prime, illustrate the thin line between triumph and disaster.

Racing also revealed a strong instinct for self-preservation. On the Continent, French, German and Italian breeding industries somehow survived two world wars... In the United States and Canada, anti-betting legislators caused hundreds of racetracks to close before 1910. In England, modern-day animal rights activists have even sought legislation to ban the Grand National.

The Turf, however, has been shrewd enough to put its house in order. Camera patrols, photo-finishes, video and drug tests for horses and riders have made it difficult to fiddle the system. Starting stalls have also made things fairer. In the year 2000, the sport is straighter than ever before.

Over the last hundred years riding styles altered as well. Until the young American Tod Sloan pulled up his irons and won a host of big races in Europe at the turn of the 19th century, jockeys rode with full-length stirrup leathers. Before long, his 'monkey-up-a-stick' style was adopted by riders all over the world. Lester Piggott added a new dimension to the Sloan crouch. Riding shorter than ever, the enigmatic maestro broke every record in the book.

Years ago, horses were trained and campaigned far harder than they are today. The 18th century champion, Eclipse, once contested two four-mile heats in a single day: Lammtarra, the 1995 Arc de Triomphe and Derby winner, ran only four times in his entire life. Air travel has widened racing's frontiers. It has never been easier to correlate international form. Raids by European horses on valuable prizes in Hong Kong, Japan and Australia are regular occurrences. Incredibly, the world's richest race is now held in the Arab emirate of Dubai.

Racing remains a game of chance played out in a theatre of dreams. As always, the quickest way to financial ruin is to back slow horses. And, while a Derby winner can still be bought for a song, money and blue-blooded breeding are no guarantees of success. The most expensive yearling ever bought at public auction failed to land a single race.

Einführung

Obwohl nach wie vor fest in der Tradition verwurzelt, hat der Pferderennsport im 20. Jahrhundert größere Veränderungen erfahren. Zwar gehören Frack und Zylinder immer noch zur Kleiderordnung für die Männer beim Royal Ascot – ganz so wie in den Tagen König Edwards VII. Auch der Aufzug der Jockeys sieht mit Seidenhemd, Reiterhose und Stiefeln noch so aus wie seit eh und je. Im Unterschied zu den zweibeinigen Athleten laufen die Pferde jedoch heute kaum schneller als noch vor 100 Jahren. Die Preise für Rassepferde sind indes in die Höhe galoppiert und ein Vollblüter stellt heutzutage eine nicht zu unterschätzende Wertanlage dar. Das Pferderennen hat sich weltweit, über den reinen Sport hinaus, zu einem großen Geschäft entwickelt. Aus dem „Sport der Könige" wurde der Sport der Wüstenprinzen. So sind die arabischen Ölscheichs zu Beginn des neuen Jahrtausends die prominentesten Pferdebesitzer auf der Bühne des internationalen Reitsports.

Das Pferderennen des 20. Jahrhunderts wartete mit zahlreichen Champions und Helden auf: Man erinnere sich an Red Rum, dreifacher Sieger der Grand National. Oder an Ribot, den italienischen Champion der 1950er Jahre. Nicht zu vergessen Sea Bird II – den wohl herausragendsten Sieger des Derbys aller Zeiten – und Secretariat, legendärer Gewinner der amerikanischen Triple Crown in den 1970er Jahren. Sie alle eroberten die Herzen des begeisterten Publikums. Natürlich spielten auch die tragischen Verlierer ihre Rolle: So zum Beispiel Devon Loch, das Hindernisrennpferd der Königin Mutter, als es – den Sieg in der 1956er Grand National vor Augen – auf unerklärliche Weise stürzte. Oder Derby-Sieger Shergar, in der Blüte seines Lebens entführt und auf grausame Weise hingerichtet; Beispiele, die zeigen, wie schmal der Grat zwischen Triumph und Katastrophe sein kann.

Das Pferderennen hat immer auch einen starken Selbsterhaltungstrieb offenbart: Auf dem europäischen Festland, in Frankreich, Deutschland und Italien, gelang es den Zuchtbetrieben, trotz aller Widrigkeiten zwei Weltkriege zu überstehen. In den Vereinigten Staaten und in Kanada führten Verordnungen gegen das Wetten dazu, dass um 1910 Hunderte von Rennbahnen geschlossen wurden. Und in England kämpft die heutige Tierschutzbewegung gar dafür, die Grand National per Gesetz zu verbieten. Der Pferderennsport ist an diesen Herausforderungen gewachsen – Kameraüberwachung, Fotofinish, Dopingtests und Videotestate von Pferd und Reiter haben Manipulationen erschwert. Seit der Einführung von Startboxen wurden die Rennen zudem gerechter. Im Jahr 2000 stellt sich der Pferdesport „sauberer" dar, als jemals zuvor.

Im Laufe der letzten 100 Jahre haben sich auch die Reitstile verändert: Jockeys ritten in langen Leder-Steigriemen, bis um die Jahrhundertwende der junge Amerikaner Tod Sloan die Bühne betrat, den Steigbügel nach oben versetzte und eine Serie großer europäischer Rennen gewann. Rasch wurde diese „Stehendhocke" von Reitern weltweit übernommen. Der große, rätselhafte Meister Lester Piggott verkürzte die Steigriemen noch weiter als Sloan und brach in der Folge alle erdenklichen Rekorde.

In früheren Zeiten wurde den Pferden in Training und Wettkampf weit mehr abverlangt als heute. Eclipse, Champion des 18. Jahrhunderts, musste einst zwei Vier-Meilen-Rennen an einem einzigen Tag bestreiten. Dagegen lief der Sieger im 1995er Arc de Triomphe, Lammtara, in seinem ganzen Leben nur vier Mal.

Die Luftfahrt hat nicht unwesentlich dazu beigetragen, die Grenzen des Pferderennens zu erweitern: Nie war es leichter, mit dem internationalen Standard Schritt zu halten. Regelmäßig nehmen europäische Pferde an hoch dotierten Rennen in Hongkong, Japan und Australien teil. Und das Rennen mit dem weltweit höchsten Preisgeld findet inzwischen in Dubai in den Vereinigten Arabischen Emiraten statt – so unglaublich das auch klingen mag.

Das Pferderennen ist und bleibt ein Glücksspiel, ausgetragen im Theater der Träume. Nach wie vor ist der sicherste Weg in den finanziellen Ruin, auf das falsche Pferd zu setzen. Und obwohl ein Derby-Sieger immer noch käuflich ist, geben Geld und Blaublüter-Zucht bei weitem keine Erfolgsgarantie. Der teuerste Einjährige, der je bei einer Auktion erstanden wurde, konnte kein einziges Rennen gewinnen.

Introduction

Même si les courses de chevaux restent résolument ancrées dans la tradition, elles ont été l'objet d'importants bouleversements au cours du XXᵉ siècle. Hauts-de-forme et queues-de-pie sont toujours de mise sur les champs de course de Royal Ascot, comme au temps du roi Édouard VII. Les casaques, les culottes et les bottes des jockeys sont, à peu de choses près, restées les mêmes que par le passé. Pourtant, à la différence de celles des athlètes humains, les chevaux ne courent pas plus vite qu'il y a cent ans. Le prix des bêtes de race a grimpé en flèche : aujourd'hui, un pur-sang représente une valeur marchande considérable. À l'échelle de la planète, les courses ne constituent plus seulement un sport, elles sont devenues une activité lucrative à part entière. Le sport favori des têtes couronnées est à présent le divertissement préféré des princes du désert et les cheiks arabes et rois du pétrole sont, en ce début de millénaire, les principaux propriétaires de chevaux sur la scène internationale des courses.

Au XXᵉ siècle, le monde équestre a connu nombre de champions et de héros parmi lesquels Red Rum, trois fois vainqueur du Grand National ; Ribot, le champion italien des années cinquante ; Sea Bird II, vainqueur du Derby d'une classe inégalée, et Secretariat, le cheval américain qui a gagné le Triple Crown dans les années soixante-dix. Tous ont suscité la ferveur d'un public enthousiaste. Sans oublier, bien sûr, les perdants tragiques, qui rappellent combien la gloire est fragile : Devon Loch, le spécialiste du steeple-chase de la reine mère qui, en 1956, chuta de manière incompréhensible sur le plat alors que le Grand National ne pouvait plus lui échapper ou encore Shergar, vainqueur du Derby, qui fut kidnappé et dont la carrière prometteuse fut brisée net en pleine fleur de l'âge.

Pour survivre, le monde des courses a dû faire preuve de la plus grande ténacité. En Europe continentale, les haras d'Allemagne, de France et d'Italie ont résisté vaille que vaille à deux guerres mondiales. Aux États-Unis et au Canada, avant 1910, les lois interdisant les paris ont entraîné la fermeture de centaines de champs de course. En Angleterre enfin, les associations de défense des animaux ont fait tout leur possible pour obtenir l'interdiction du Grand National. Toutefois, le monde du turf a fait preuve de suffisamment d'astuce pour qu'évolue la profession. Caméras mobiles, photographies sur la ligne d'arrivée, vidéo et contrôles anti-dopage des jockeys comme des chevaux ont considérablement compliqué la tâche aux éventuels tricheurs. L'utilisation de stalles au départ a également rendu les courses moins aléatoires. À l'aube de l'an 2 000, les courses sont plus équitables que jamais.

Les styles de monte ont également évolué tout au long des cent dernières années. Il a fallu que l'Américain Tod Sloan raccourcisse ses étriers, vers le début du siècle dernier, remportant de nombreuses courses de premier plan en Europe, pour que les jockeys se décident à en faire de même. Très vite, son style de monte accroupi devait être adopté par l'ensemble des jockeys. Lester Piggott alla encore plus loin que Sloan et le mystérieux maître, adoptant des courroies plus courtes que jamais, battit tous les records.

Par le passé, le rythme d'entraînement et de compétition des chevaux était nettement plus intense qu'aujourd'hui. À titre d'exemple, Eclipse, un champion du XVIIIᵉ siècle, disputa la même journée deux courses de 4 miles (près de 7 kilomètres) chacune tandis que Lammtarra, le vainqueur du Grand Prix de l'Arc de Triomphe en 1995, ne participa en tout et pour tout qu'à quatre courses durant sa carrière. De plus, le développement du transport aérien a offert davantage de possibilités, même si l'organisation d'épreuves à l'échelon international ne fut jamais tâche aisée. Il n'est toutefois pas rare de voir des chevaux européens remporter d'importantes épreuves à Hong-Kong, au Japon ou en Australie. Enfin, bien que cela paraisse stupéfiant, la course la mieux dotée se tient aujourd'hui dans l'émirat arabe de Dubaï.

Les courses constituent bien un jeu de hasard joué dans un théâtre de rêve. Le plus sûr moyen de faire faillite reste de miser sur les chevaux les plus lents. Et, s'il est possible d'acquérir le futur vainqueur du Derby pour trois fois rien, à l'inverse l'acquisition d'un cheval de race à un prix exorbitant ne présente aucune garantie absolue de succès. Le yearling le plus cher jamais acheté lors d'une vente aux enchères n'a pas remporté la moindre course.

1. An era of elegance
Das Zeitalter der Eleganz
Une époque élégante

An exemplar of the Corinthian ideal. The Victorian amateur rider, Captain Roddy Owen, who won the 1892 Grand National on Father O'Flynn. Sadly, Owen, then a major, died three years later after a bout of cholera while on active service in Egypt with his regiment.

Ein Musterbeispiel für das korinthische Ideal: der viktorianische Amateur-Jockey Captain Roddy Owen, auf Father O'Flynn, Sieger der Grand National von 1892. Owen, der damals Major war, verstarb drei Jahre später auf traurige Weise. Mit seinem Regiment im aktiven Dienst in Ägypten, fiel er der Cholera zum Opfer.

Un modèle de l'idéal corinthien. À l'époque victorienne, le capitaine Roddy Owen, jockey amateur, remporte le Grand National en 1892 sur Father O'Flynn. Hélas, trois ans plus tard en Égypte, Owen, alors devenu commandant, devait mourir des suites d'une crise de choléra durant le service actif avec son régiment.

The carefree Edwardian days of the first decade of the 20th century were, in every sense, the lull before the great storm. King Edward VII won the 1909 Derby with Minoru but would be dead before the next Derby was run. 1910 saw the end of a decade and the end of an era: war and politics would soon put a stop to all the frivolity. The suffragette Emily Davison died under the hooves of George V's horse, Anmer, in the 1913 Derby. A year later Europe embarked on the Great War and, like most other sports, racing took a back seat. Trainers, owners, jockeys and stable lads went to the trenches. Many never returned. In the United States anti-gambling laws persuaded many racing professionals to ply their trade in Europe: Tod Sloan, the Reiff brothers and Danny Maher thrilled the crowds with their riding skills. But the new arrivals also imported a more sinister element: with the introduction of the hypodermic syringe, American dopers relieved British bookmakers of a staggering £2 million in the first four years of the century. Throughout the good times and the bad times, however, there were great horses. Three of the finest fillies in racing history, Sceptre, Signorinetta and Pretty Polly dominated the first decade and The Tetrarch, the fastest two-year-old ever to race, pulverised his contemporaries in the 1913 season.

Die Sorglosigkeit der ersten Dekade des 20. Jahrhunderts – die Zeit König Edwards VII. – war in jeder Hinsicht nur eine Ruhe vor dem Sturm. Noch 1909 gewann König Edward VII. das Derby mit seinem Pferd Minoru. Das nächste Derby erlebte Edward nicht mehr. So markierte das Jahr 1910 über den Abschluss einer Dekade hinaus das Ende einer Ära: Krieg und Politik sollten der Leichtigkeit des Seins schon bald ein Ende setzen. Die Frauenrechtlerin Emily Davison starb unter den Hufen des Pferdes von Georg V., Anmer, im Derby von 1913. Ein Jahr darauf brach in Europa der Erste Weltkrieg aus und der Pferdesport – wie die meisten anderen Sportarten auch – spielte fortan eine untergeordnete Rolle. Trainer, Pferdebesitzer und Stalljungen zogen in die Schützengräben, aus denen viele nicht wiederkehrten. Die amerikanischen Verordnungen gegen das Wetten bewogen zahlreiche Aktive des Pferdesports, ihr Glück in Europa zu suchen. Darunter Tod Sloan, die Gebrüder Reiff und Danny Maher, die das Publikum mit ihren Fähigkeiten zu Pferde in Atem hielten. Doch die Welle von Neuankömmlingen schwemmte auch finstere

Kräfte an: Nach Einführung der Injektions-Spritze wurden durch das Doping amerikanischer Pferde britische Buchmacher in den ersten vier Jahren des Jahrhunderts um sage und schreibe zwei Millionen Pfund erleichtert. Wie gut oder schlecht die Zeit auch gewesen sein mag – sie brachte große Pferde hervor. Mit Sceptre, Signorinetta und Pretty Polly dominierten drei der besten Stutenfohlen in der Geschichte des Pferderennsports das erste Jahrzehnt, und in der Saison von 1913 galoppierte der schnellste Zweijährige aller Zeiten – The Tetrarch – seinen Zeitgenossen um Längen davon.

Le règne d'Édouard, durant la première décennie du XXe siècle, fut marquée par l'insouciance et constitua à tous égards la dernière période de calme avant la tempête. Édouard VII remporta le Derby en 1909 avec Minoru mais il mourut avant de pouvoir assister au Derby suivant. L'année 1910 marquait donc la fin d'une époque en même temps que celle d'une décennie : la politique et la guerre ne tarderaient pas à sonner le glas de toute frivolité. Lors du Derby de 1913, la suffragette Emily Davison succombait sous les sabots d'Anmer, monture du roi George V. Un an plus tard débutait la Grande Guerre, reléguant les courses à l'arrière-plan, à l'instar de la plupart des autres sports. Entraîneurs, propriétaires, jockeys et garçons d'écurie se retrouvèrent dans les tranchées et nombreux furent ceux qui ne revinrent jamais. Aux États-Unis, l'adoption d'une réglementation visant à empêcher les paris amena la plupart des professionnels à transférer leurs activités en Europe : les talents de Tod Sloan, des frères Reiff et de Danny Maher soulevèrent ainsi l'enthousiasme des foules. Mais les nouveaux venus introduisaient aussi des pratiques plus condamnables comme celle des seringues hypodermiques. On estime que, durant les quatre premières années du siècle, les revendeurs américains parvinrent ainsi à soutirer la somme colossale de deux millions de livres sterling aux bookmakers britanniques. Cependant, dans les périodes florissantes comme dans les mauvaises passes, il y eut toujours des chevaux extraordinaires. Trois des meilleures pouliches de l'histoire des courses, Sceptre, Signorinetta et Pretty Polly dominèrent cette première décennie et, en 1913, The Tetrarch, un cheval de deux ans, allait pulvériser tous ses adversaires.

The stage is set for the world's most famous flat race. A panoramic view of Epsom on Derby Day in 1899. In the Victorian era Derby Day was a great public holiday. Parliament did not sit and it was the British Prime Minister Benjamin Disraeli who first described the Derby as the 'Blue Riband of the Turf'.

Bühne frei für das berühmteste Flachrennen der Welt. Ein Panoramablick auf das Hippodrom von Epsom am Derby-Tag des Jahres 1899. In der Viktorianischen Epoche war dieser Tag ein öffentlicher Feiertag, an dem sogar das Parlament ruhte. Der britische Premierminister Benjamin Disraeli bezeichnete das Derby einst als das „Blaue Band des Turfs".

Tout est prêt pour la plus célèbre course de plat au monde. Vue panoramique d'Epsom, un jour de Derby en 1899. Durant la période victorienne, le jour du Derby était l'occasion d'importantes réjouissances publiques. Ce jour-là, le Parlement ne siégeait pas et Benjamin Disraeli, Premier Ministre britannique, fut le premier à considérer le Derby comme « le ruban bleu du turf ».

(Above) Royal winner. King Edward VII on the right with his 1909 Derby winner, Minoru (Herbert Jones up).
(Opposite) The Chevalier Ginistrelli, owner of 1908 Derby winner Signorinetta, with Madame Lemaire de Villiers,
7 December 1911. The eccentric Italian surprised the racing community with Signorinetta's 100/1 Epsom win.

(Oben) Ein königlicher Sieger. König Edward VII. (rechts im Bild) und sein Pferd Minoru, Derby-Sieger des Jahres 1909.
Der Jockey ist Herbert Jones. (Gegenüberliegende Seite) Der Chevalier Ginistrelli, Eigentümer von Signorinetta, die
1908 das Derby gewann, mit Madame Lemaire de Villiers, 7. Dezember 1911. Der exzentrische Italiener überraschte
die Fachwelt mit Signorinettas 100/1-Sieg in Epsom.

(Ci-dessus) Un vainqueur royal. À droite, le roi Édouard VII accompagné par Minoru, le vainqueur du Derby de 1909
dont il est propriétaire monté ici par Herbert Jones. (Ci-contre) Le Chevalier Ginistrelli, propriétaire de Signorinetta, vainqueur du Derby de 1908, est accompagné de Madame Lemaire de Villiers, 7 décembre 1911. L'excentrique Italien avait
bien épaté le monde des courses en s'adjugeant la victoire à Epsom alors que son cheval n'était coté qu'à 100 contre un.

The apex of high society. Ladies display their summer finery in the Royal Box at Glorious Goodwood, July 1907. Goodwood, situated on top of the Sussex Downs, has always been one of the most beautiful racecourses in Britain.

Die Spitze der Highsociety. In der königlichen Loge von Glorious Goodwood tragen die Ladys ihren Sommerstaat zur Schau, Juli 1907. Das auf den Hügeln von Sussex gelegene Goodwood galt zu allen Zeiten als eines der schönsten Hippodrome Großbritanniens.

Le haut du panier. Les dames de la haute société font admirer leurs toilettes d'été dans la loge royale de Glorious Goodwood, au mois de juillet 1907. Goodwood, situé au sommet des collines du Sussex, constitue l'un des plus beaux hippodromes britanniques.

Jolly good boating weather. Boaters are the order of the day in the Silver Ring enclosure at Epsom on Derby Day, 1911. The Silver Ring, the cheapest enclosure on British race-courses, was so-called because in those days admission cost less than a pound.

Welch ein Sägen-haftes Wetter! „Kreissägen" bestimmten die Hutmode auf den Stehplätzen beim Epsom Derby Day des Jahres 1911. Die preiswerteste Stehplatz-Zone aller britischen Rennbahnen wurde „The Silver Ring" genannt, weil zu jener Zeit der Eintritt weniger als ein Pfund kostete.

Un temps idéal pour le canotage. Et les canotiers sont bien à l'ordre du jour pour le Derby d'Epsom, en 1911. Le Silver Ring constituait l'enceinte la moins chère des champs de course britanniques, avec un prix d'entrée inférieur à une livre sterling.

(Opposite) A celestial winner. George Stern and Sunstar return in triumph after the 1911 Derby. (Above) Stern has Sunstar beautifully positioned in second place at Tattenham Corner with three and a half furlongs to run.

(Gegenüber) Ein himmlischer Sieger. George Stern mit Sunstar nach dem Sieg beim Derby von 1911. (Oben) In der Tattenham-Kurve, zirka 700 Meter vor dem Ziel, hat Stern seinen Sunstar in die aussichtsreiche zweite Position gebracht.

(Ci-contre) Un fantastique vainqueur. C'est l'heure du triomphe pour George Stern et Sunstar, après leur victoire dans le Derby de 1911. (Ci-dessus) Stern a magnifiquement placé Sunstar en seconde position dans le virage de Tattenham, à environ 700 m de l'arrivée.

Horsepower under the bonnet. (Above) Motor cars were still rare enough to attract attention. Racegoers arrive in style for the Derby, June 1911. (Opposite) Spectators and a lone bookmaker with his betting board use a taxi cab as an impromptu grandstand at Epsom in the same year.

Pferdestärken unter der Haube. (Oben) Stilvoller Auftritt von Rennbahnbesuchern beim Epsom Derby im Juni 1911. Damals waren Automobile noch ein seltener Anblick, der Aufmerksamkeit garantierte. (Gegenüber) Zuschauer und ein einsamer Buchmacher mit seinem Wett-Stand nutzen ein Taxi als improvisierte Tribüne in Epsom im selben Jahr.

Des chevaux-vapeur sous le capot. (Ci-dessus) Les engins motorisés étaient encore rares et attiraient tous les regards. En juin 1911, pour le Derby, ces turfistes font une arrivée fort remarquée. (Ci-contre) Des spectateurs et un bookmaker isolé (avec un tableau des paris) improvisent une tribune sur ce taxi lors du Derby d'Epsom de la même année.

In the cold light of day, five stable lads educate their mounts at the starting gate on a snowy morning in 1910. Leaving the gate at speed was vital in races run over sprint distances. Hoods and woollen sheets were worn at exercise to protect the horses from freezing temperatures.

Fünf Stalljungen trainieren im kalten Tageslicht mit ihren Pferden an der Startmaschine an einem schneereichen Morgen des Jahres 1910. Ein schneller Start war bei Flachrennen über die Kurzstrecke von entscheidender Bedeutung. Mit Kapuzen und Wolldecken wurden die Pferde beim Training vor den Minustemperaturen geschützt.

Cinq garçons d'écurie entraînent leurs montures au départ, par une matinée neigeuse de 1910. Pour les courses de vitesse sur des distances courtes, il était primordial de prendre un bon départ. Lors des entraînements hivernaux, les chevaux étaient protégés par des capuchons et des couvertures de laine.

Champion racehorses. (Above) The peerless Sceptre, who won four Classics in 1902, at the Newmarket bloodstock sales, 1911. (Opposite) The Tetrarch, the fastest two-year-old ever to race. Known as 'the Spotted Wonder', the grey colt thrilled British racegoers with his blistering speed in the 1913 season.

Vierbeinige Champions. (Oben) Der unvergleichliche Sceptre bei der Vollblüter-Auktion in Newmarket, 1911. Sceptre gewann vier Klassiker des Jahres 1902. (Gegenüber) The Tetrarch, das schnellste zweijährige Rennpferd aller Zeiten. Das Schimmelfohlen, bekannt unter dem Namen „das gepunktete Wunder", hielt das Rennpublikum in der Saison 1913 mit seinem unwiderstehlichen Galopp in Atem.

Des chevaux gagnants. (Ci-dessus) Sceptre, le champion hors pair qui remporta quatre classiques en 1902, lors d'une vente de pur-sang à Newmarket, en 1911. (Ci-contre) The Tetrarch, le cheval de deux ans le plus rapide de tous les temps, était également surnommé « la merveille tachetée ». Par son galop époustouflant, le poulain gris enthousiasma les turfistes britanniques durant la saison de 1913.

Champion riders. (Opposite) Lancashire-born Steve Donoghue, who rode six Derby winners. (Left) Tod Sloan. (Above) Danny Maher (centre, smiling at the camera). Sloan and Maher were two great American jockeys who rode in Europe in the early part of the 20th century.

Zweibeinige Champions. (Gegenüber) Der aus Lancashire stammende sechsfache Derby-Gewinner Steve Donoghue. (Links) Tod Sloan. (Oben) Danny Maher (Bildmitte, in die Kamera lächelnd). Sloan und Maher waren zwei große amerikanische Jockeys, die zu Beginn des 20. Jahrhunderts Rennen in Europa bestritten.

Des jockeys gagnants. (Ci-contre) Steve Donoghue, natif du Lancashire, remporta six fois le Derby. (À gauche) Tod Sloan. (Ci-dessus) Danny Maher (au centre, souriant au photographe). Sloan et Maher, deux fameux jockeys américains, exerçaient leur talent en Europe au début du XXᵉ siècle.

Black Ascot. (Above) Racegoers wore black at the 1910 Royal Meeting in memory of King Edward VII who had died earlier in the year. (Opposite) The Marquess of Londonderry with the Countess of Derby, wife of the leading owner, the 17th Earl, and her daughter, Lady Victoria Stanley, at Black Ascot.

Black Ascot. (Oben) Zum Gedenken an den kurz zuvor verstorbenen König Edward VII. trugen die Zuschauer beim Royal Meeting von 1910 schwarz. (Gegenüber) Der Marquis von Londonderry mit der Gräfin von Derby – Gattin des führenden Besitzers, des 17. Earl von Derby, – und ihrer Tochter Lady Victoria Stanley beim „schwarzen Ascot".

Black Ascot. (Ci-dessus) Les turfistes sont vêtus de noir pour le meeting royal organisé en 1910 à la mémoire du roi Édouard VII, disparu quelques mois plus tôt. (Ci-contre) À Ascot, le marquis de Londonderry est accompagné de la comtesse de Derby, épouse d'un des plus grands propriétaires, le 17ᵉ comte de Derby, et de la fille de cette dernière, Lady Victoria Stanley.

(Above) French master. George Stern (left), the outstanding jockey, in France in the first quarter of the century, on the way to weigh-in with a colleague, 1912. (Opposite) French chic. Four immaculately clad racegoers show why Paris has always been the capital of the fashion world, 1907.

(Oben) Französischer Meister. George Stern (links), herausragender Jockey Frankreichs im ersten Viertel des 20. Jahrhunderts, auf dem Weg zum Wiegen mit einem Kollegen im Jahre 1912. (Gegenüber) Französischer Chic. Diese vier makellos gekleideten Zuschauer des Jahres 1907 zeigen, dass Paris schon immer die Hauptstadt der Mode war.

(Ci-dessus) Le maître français. George Stern, à gauche, remarquable jockey français durant le premier quart de siècle, se dirige vers la pesée en compagnie d'un collègue, 1912. (Ci-contre) Le chic français. L'élégance de ces quatre amateurs de courses montre bien que Paris a toujours été la « capitale mondiale de la mode », 1907.

It is all about winning. Packed grandstand, packed race course and Eton Boy races clear of the field to take the 1912 Royal Hunt Cup. The four-day Royal Ascot fixture in flaming June has always been the highlight of the British summer social season.

Nur der Sieg zählt. Gleichermaßen dichtes Gedränge auf Haupttribüne und Turf beim Royal Hunt Cup von 1912. Hier setzt sich Eton Boy vom Feld ab und reitet dem Sieg entgegen. Das viertägige Royal Ascot Meeting in der brütenden Junihitze ist seit jeher gesellschaftlicher Höhepunkt der britischen Sommersaison.

La victoire est au bout. Une course groupée devant des tribunes combles, et Eton Boy se dégage pour remporter la Royal Hunt Cup de 1912. La manifestation de Royal Ascot, d'une durée de quatre jours sous le soleil de juin, constitue depuis toujours le grand événement mondain de l'été en Grande-Bretagne.

Summer comes to the Surrey Downs, 1911. (Above) Derby Day has always offered racegoers an opportunity to dress up. A lady punter smilingly places a bet with bookmaker Harry Hopkins. (Opposite) Bookmakers' advertising boards display the latest prices on the Downs in the centre of Epsom racecourse.

Der Sommer des Jahres 1911 hält Einzug auf die Hügel von Surrey. (Oben) Der Tag des Derby bot zu allen Zeiten Anlass, sich in Schale zu werfen. Eine weibliche Glücksspielerin platziert ihre Wette beim Buchmacher Harry Hopkins. (Gegenüber) Die Werbetafeln der Buchmacher im Zentrum der Rennbahn von Epsom zeigen die aktuellen Wettquoten.

Premiers jours d'été sur les collines du Surrey, 1911. (Ci-dessus) Le jour du Derby est toujours une bonne occasion de sortir ses plus beaux habits. Ici, une joueuse place ses paris auprès du bookmaker Harry Hopkins. (Ci-contre) Les panneaux publicitaires des bookmakers affichant les dernières cotes, sur les collines situées au milieu du champ de course d'Epsom.

The lull. A stable lad leads King George V's horse, Anmer, and jockey, Herbert Jones, in the pre-race parade before the Derby, 4 June 1913. George V was not as keen on racing as his father, but took a great interest in the Royal Stud at Sandringham. However, he won the 1928 1,000 Guineas with Scuttle.

Die Ruhe. Ein Stalljunge führt Anmer – das Pferd von König George V. – und Jockey Herbert Jones vor dem Derby auf die Promenade, 4. Juni 1913. George V. war weniger angetan vom Pferderennen als sein Vater, sein Interesse galt eher dem königlichen Gestüt von Sandringham. Dennoch gewann er 1928 die 1 000 Guineas mit Scuttle.

Le calme. Un garçon d'écurie conduit Anmer, le cheval du roi George V, et son jockey Herbert Jones, pour la présentation précédant le Derby du 4 juin 1913. George V n'était pas un amateur de courses aussi fervent que son père mais portait un vif intérêt aux haras royaux de Sandringham. Il remporta toutefois le 1 000 Guinées de 1928 avec Scuttle.

The storm. Minutes later, disaster strikes when the suffragette Emily Davison throws herself under the feet of the King's horse at Tattenham Corner. Although Emily Davison was fatally injured, Anmer and Herbert Jones miraculously escaped unscathed.

Der Sturm. Minuten später kommt es zur Katastrophe, als sich die Suffragette Emily Davison in der Tattenham-Kurve unter das königliche Pferd wirft. Davison wurde tödlich verletzt, Anmer und Jockey Herbert Jones jedoch blieben auf wundersame Weise unversehrt.

La tempête. Quelques minutes plus tard, la suffragette Emily Davison se jette sous les sabots de la monture royale, au niveau du virage de Tattenham. Cette dernière fut mortellement blessée, mais Anmer et Herbert Jones sortirent miraculeusement indemnes de l'accident.

There is no such thing as a racing certainty… The 100/1 outsider Aboyeur, Edwin Piper up, returning to unsaddle after finishing second in the 1913 Suffragette Derby. Aboyeur was later awarded the race after the stewards disqualified the winner, Craganour.

Nachher ist man immer klüger… Der 100/1-Außenseiter Aboyeur mit Jockey Edwin Piper auf dem Weg zum Absatteln nach ihrem zweiten Platz beim tragischen Derby von 1913. Später wurde Aboyeur sogar der Sieg zuerkannt, weil der ursprüngliche Gewinner Craganour von der Rennleitung disqualifiziert wurde.

Aucune certitude dans le monde des courses… Aboyeur, outsider à cent contre un monté ici par Edwin Piper, se prépare à être dessellé après sa seconde place dans le Derby Suffragette de 1913. Un peu plus tard, Aboyeur allait même se voir attribuer la victoire suite à la disqualification de Craganour.

Riding roughshod. A nail-biting finish for one of the roughest and most controversial Derbys ever run. Aboyeur (second from the left) was beaten by a head by the blinkered Craganour (nearest camera), ridden by the American rider Johnny Reiff.

Mit Haken und Ösen. Das verbissen umkämpfte Finish bei einem der härtesten und umstrittensten Derbys aller Zeiten. Aboyeur (Zweiter von links) wird um einen Kopf von Craganour geschlagen (mit Scheuklappen, ganz vorn im Bild). Im Sattel: der amerikanische Jockey Johnny Reiff.

Une arrivée cavalière. Arrivée dans un mouchoir de poche pour ce Derby qui reste comme l'un des plus controversé de tous les temps. Aboyeur, le second cheval à partir de la gauche, est battu d'une tête par Craganour (le cheval équipé d'œillères au premier plan), monté par le jockey américain Johnny Reiff.

Paddock talk. (Above) The 17th Earl of Derby (third from right) assesses the prospects of a runner with jockey George Bellhouse in the paddock, 1916. (Opposite) A persistent gypsy woman with baby in arms tries to sell brushes to two disinterested high society racegoers at Royal Ascot, June 1914.

Koppel-Gespräche. (Oben) Der 17. Earl von Derby (Dritter von rechts) informiert sich auf dem Sattelplatz bei Jockey George Bellhouse über die Aussichten eines Rennpferdes, 1916. (Gegenüber) Royal Ascot, Juni 1914. Eine hartnäckige Zigeunerin mit einem Kind auf dem Arm beim Versuch, zwei eher desinteressierten Zuschauern aus der Highsociety einen Besen zu verkaufen.

Discussion au paddock. (Ci-dessus) Le 17ᵉ comte de Derby (troisième en partant de la droite) évalue les chances d'un partant en compagnie du jockey George Bellhouse dans le paddock, 1916. (Ci-contre) Royal Ascot, juin 1914. Une gitane portant un bébé dans ses bras essaie avec insistance de vendre des brosses à deux amateurs de courses de la haute société, parfaitement impassibles.

The luck of the Irish. (Above) Horse and rider in full flight at a treacherous Irish bank.
(Opposite) Lord and Lady Shaftesbury use a bench to obtain a better view of the action at
Punchestown, Eire, April 1913. Punchestown was Edward VII's favourite Irish racecourse.

Das Glück der Iren. (Oben) Ross und Reiter in vollem Flug über ein heimtückisches Hindernis.
(Gegenüber) Lord und Lady Shaftesbury suchen auf einer Bank den besseren Überblick über
das Renngeschehen im irischen Punchestown, April 1913. Punchestown war die bevorzugte
Rennbahn Edwards VII. in Irland.

La chance sur l'obstacle irlandais. (Ci-dessus) Le cheval et le cavalier sont en plein effort sur ce
talus irlandais fort trompeur. (Ci-contre) Lord et Lady Shaftesbury sont juchés sur un banc
pour mieux voir la course à Punchestown (République d'Irlande), l'épreuve hippique favorite
d'Édouard VII, avril 1913.

Jumping for joy. A fascinated crowd watches the field take a huge open ditch in the 1912 Grand National at Aintree. The eventual winner was Jerry M, ridden by Ernie Piggott, the grandfather of Lester Piggott, the renowned flat jockey of another era. Seven years later, Ernie won the National again on Pocthlyn.

Freudensprünge. Das faszinierte Publikum verfolgt den Übersprung des großen Grabens bei der 1912er Grand National in Aintree. Der spätere Sieger Jerry M wurde von Ernie Piggott geritten, dessen Enkel Lester Piggott später bei Flachrennen zu Ruhm kommen sollte. Sieben Jahre danach gewann Ernie erneut die Grand National, diesmal auf Pocthlyn.

Un saut pour le plaisir... du public! Le public, fasciné, regarde les concurrents affronter cet obstacle imposant, lors du Grand National de 1912, à Aintree. Le vainqueur de la course fut Jerry M, monté par Ernie Piggott, le grand-père de Lester Piggott, lequel deviendra plus tard un jockey célèbre. Sept ans plus tard, Ernie remportait à nouveau le National sur Pocthlyn.

Heading for a fall. The enormous and unforgiving Grand National fences rarely allow mistakes by horse or rider. A vivid (and painful) reminder as several runners hit the deck in a pile-up at Aintree. Nowadays, the National fences have been severely modified, with the result that there are generally fewer falls and more finishers in the 4½ mile race.

Kurz vor dem Fall. Die gewaltigen und gnadenlosen Hürden der Grand National bestrafen den kleinsten Fehler von Pferd oder Reiter. Das Bild von einem Massensturz in Aintree führt dies eindrucksvoll und schmerzhaft vor Augen. Inzwischen wurden die Zäune so weit entschärft, dass bei dem Viereinhalb-Meilen-Rennen (7240m) die Pferde seltener stürzen und häufiger ins Ziel kommen.

Droit vers la chute. Les haies imposantes du Grand National ne pardonnent pas la moindre erreur des chevaux ou des cavaliers. Cette chute collective à Aintree, vient le rappeler aux concurrents, à leurs dépens. Aujourd'hui, les haies du National ont été totalement remodelées, ce qui a permis de diminuer le nombre de chutes et d'augmenter celui des participants parvenant au terme de 7240 mètres de course.

The fulfilment of a lifetime's ambition. The popular racehorse owner Lord Glanely, who was affectionately nicknamed 'Old Guts & Gaiters' by racegoers, leads in his 1919 Derby winner Grand Parade, ridden by Fred Templeman. Mounted policemen keep a watchful eye on the proceedings.

Am Ziel eines Lebenstraums. Der populäre Pferdebesitzer Lord Glanely wurde vom Rennbahn-publikum liebevoll „Old Guts & Gaiters" getauft (der Alte mit Mumm und Gamaschen). Hier führt er seinen Derby-Sieger von 1919, Grand Parade, und dessen Jockey Fred Templeman zum Stall. Berittene Polizisten werfen ein wachsames Auge auf die Szene.

Le rêve de toute une vie. Lord Glanely, le très populaire propriétaire de chevaux de course, surnommé affectueusement par les amateurs de course «Old Guts & Gaiters» (le Père Courage chaussé de guêtres), mène Grand Parade, le vainqueur du Grand National de 1919, monté par Fred Templeman. Des policiers à cheval surveillent la scène de près.

2. Roaring away
Wilde Zeiten
Les années folles

A bird's-eye view of the Derby. Mr and Mrs Henry Mond and Mr G Cannon watch the 1922 race from the roof of a motor car. The easy four lengths' winner was Lord Woolavington's Captain Cuttle, ridden by Steve Donoghue and trained by Fred Darling.

Das Derby aus der Vogelperspektive. Mr. und Mrs. Henry Mond und Mr. G. Cannon verfolgen das 1922er Rennen vom Dach eines Wagens aus. Lord Woolavingtons Captain Cuttle, geritten von Steve Donoghue und trainiert von Fred Darling, siegte souverän mit vier Längen Vorsprung.

Vue d'ensemble du Derby. M et Mme Henry Mond, accompagnés de M G. Cannon assistent à l'édition de 1922 depuis le toit d'une automobile. Captain Cuttle, le cheval de Lord Woolavington monté pour l'occasion par Steve Donoghue et entraîné par Fred Darling, devait l'emporter facilement avec quatre longueurs d'avance.

Racing recovered remarkably quickly after the First World War. 'Come on, Steve' was the perennial cry at Epsom as huge crowds, basking in the euphoria of peace, urged the popular jockey, Steve Donoghue, to four Derby triumphs in the Roaring Twenties. In a golden decade for British racing, the flying filly Mumtaz Mahal brought memories of her brilliant sire, The Tetrarch, flooding back in 1923. The sickly Humorist was nursed by Donoghue to a courageous and poignant Derby win; the strapping Easter Hero took the 1929 Cheltenham Gold Cup in a canter; Fred Darling's Beckhampton stable was the most powerful in the land. The French and Americans had cause to celebrate as well. Epinard crossed the Channel to land a massive gamble in the 1923 Stewards' Cup. The mighty Man o' War bestrode American racing like a colossus, winning twenty of his twenty-one starts. Gordon Richards won the first of many Jockeys' Championships in 1925 and the Stewards of the Jockey Club withdrew Charlie Smirke's riding licence for preventing a hot favourite from starting at Gatwick in 1928. The Tote, whose profits are returned to racing, operated for the first time on a British racecourse at Newmarket in 1929.

Nach dem Ersten Weltkrieg erholte sich der Pferderennsport bemerkenswert schnell. Begleitet von dem legendären Schlachtruf „Come on, Steve" und beflügelt von der Euphorie über den neuen Frieden, trieben die Publikumsmassen in Epsom den populären Jockey Steve Donoghue zu vier Derby-Siegen in den Goldenen Zwanzigern. Es war ein goldenes Jahrzehnt für den britischen Pferderennsport: Mumtaz Mahal, das „fliegende Fohlen", ließ im Jahre 1923 die Erinnerung an seinen großartigen Zuchthengst The Tetrarch wieder lebendig werden. Das kränkliche Pferd Humorist wurde dank der Pflege von Donoghue zum tapferen und beherzten Derby-Sieger. Der stramme Easter Hero holte mühelos den Cheltenham Gold Cup des Jahres 1929. Zu jener Zeit war Fred Darlings Beckhampton-Stall der erfolgreichste im ganzen Land. Aber auch die Franzosen und Amerikaner hatten Grund zu feiern: Epinard überquerte den Ärmelkanal und erzielte gigantische Quoten im Stewards' Cup von 1923. Der unwiderstehliche Man o' War überstrahlte mit 20 Siegen bei 21 Starts den gesamten amerikanischen Pferderennsport. 1925 gewann Gordon Richards das erste seiner zahlreichen Jockey-Championate. Die Verantwortlichen des Jockey Clubs entzogen Charlie Smirke 1928 die Reitlizenz, weil er den Start eines großen Favoriten in Gatwick verhinderte. Im Jahre 1929 kam in Newmarket erstmals auf einer britischen Rennbahn das Prinzip des Totalisators (im Volksmund: „The Tote") zum Einsatz, durch das die Wettgewinne in den Sport zurückfließen.

Après la Première Guerre mondiale, les courses reprirent très vite de l'ampleur. À Epsom, où, dans les années vingt, se pressait une foule considérable, baignant dans l'euphorie de la paix retrouvée, les supporters du très populaire jockey Steve Donoghue l'encourageaient aux cris de «Allez, Steve» à chacune de ses quatre victoires au Derby. Une décennie en or pour les courses britanniques : la pouliche Mumtaz Mahal revenait en force en 1923, rappelant qu'elle était la digne héritière de The Tetrarch, son géniteur. Humorist, un cheval souffreteux, bénéficiait de toutes les attentions de Donoghue qui l'amenait à la victoire au Derby au terme d'une course courageuse et pleine d'émotions. En 1929, c'était Easter Hero, un cheval bien bâti, qui remportait haut la main la Gold Cup de Cheltenham. Incontestablement, l'écurie de Fred Darling, à Beckhampton, surclassait alors toutes les autres écuries britanniques. Les Français et les Américains avaient eux aussi des raisons de se réjouir. En effet, le Français Epinard traversait la Manche pour gagner un pari risqué lors de la Stewards' Cup de 1923 et l'imposant Man o' War dominait de toute sa puissance le monde des courses américaines, en remportant 20 victoires pour 21 participations. Gordon Richards remportait en 1925 le premier d'une longue série des Championnats des jockeys, tandis qu'en 1928 les responsables du Jockey Club retiraient sa licence de jockey à Charlie Smirke qui avait empêché un des chevaux favoris de se présenter au départ à Gatwick. En 1929, à Newmarket, «The Tote», dont les bénéfices devaient revenir aux courses, faisait son apparition pour la première fois sur un champ de courses britannique.

(Opposite)
Jockey Joe Childs
unsaddles the 1926
Derby winner
Coronach. (Right)
Smiles of victory.
Mrs Hugh Kershaw
leads in her 1922
Grand National win-
ner Music Hall and
jockey Bilbie Rees.

(Gegenüber)
Der Jockey Joe
Childs beim Ab-
satteln des Derby-
Gewinners von 1926
Coronach. (Rechts)
Das Lächeln der
Sieger. Mrs. Hugh
Kershaw führt ihr
Pferd Music Hall
mitsamt Jockey
Bilbie Rees nach
dem Sieg bei der
1922er Grand
National zum Stall.

(Ci-contre)
Le jockey Joe Childs
retire la selle de
Coronach, vainqueur
du Derby en 1926.
(À droite) Le sourire
de la victoire. Après
sa victoire dans le
Grand National de
1922, Mme Hugh
Kershaw ramène
son cheval Music
Hall, monté par
Bilbie Rees.

Small is beautiful. Two apprentices who would later become top flat jockeys. Charlie Smirke (left) and Chubb Leach carry their saddles after riding in the City and Suburban Handicap at the Epsom Spring Meeting in April 1923.

Klein, aber oho. Zwei Nachwuchsreiter, die später bedeutende Jockeys im Flachrennen werden sollten: Charlie Smirke (links) und Chubb Leach tragen ihre Sattel nach ihrem Ritt beim City and Suburban Handicap im Rahmen des Frühjahrsmeetings von Epsom, im April 1923.

Tout ce qui est petit est joli. Deux apprentis jockeys en herbe destinés à devenir un jour parmi les meilleurs spécialistes des courses de plat. Charlie Smirke (à gauche) et Chubb Leach portent leur selle après avoir participé au handicap de Londres et de la banlieue lors du meeting de printemps d'Epsom, en avril 1923.

Two of a kind. Binoculars give two identically attired young racegoers the opportunity to view the action at close quarters on Derby Day, 1921. Perhaps they were looking at the winner, Humorist, and every small boy's hero, Steve Donoghue.

Gleich und Gleich gesellt sich gern. Diese zwei jungen Freunde des Pferderennens sind nicht nur identisch gekleidet. Beide bedienen sich ihrer Ferngläser, um das Geschehen am Derby Day des Jahres 1921 näher zu betrachten. Vielleicht haben sie den siegreichen Humorist und den damaligen Helden eines jeden Jungen, Steve Donoghue, im Visier.

À l'identique. Ces deux amateurs habillés à l'identique suivent le Derby de 1921 de près grâce à leurs jumelles. Peut-être suivent-ils la course du vainqueur Humorist, monté par Steve Donoghue, l'idole de tous les petits garçons.

(Above) Poetry in motion. Steve Donoghue and Captain Cuttle easily winning the 1922 Derby. (Opposite) The long arms of the law. A caped policemen protects the top-hatted 17th Earl of Derby and jockey Tommy Weston after Sansovino's 1924 Derby triumph.

(Oben) Eine Bewegungsstudie voller Poesie. Steve Donoghue und Captain Cuttle auf dem Weg zu einem sicheren Derby-Sieg im Jahr 1922. (Gegenüber) Der lange Arm des Gesetzes. Das Regencape schützt den Polizisten, der Polizist schützt den Zylinder tragenden 17. Earl von Derby nebst Pferd Sansovino und Jockey Tommy Weston nach ihrem triumphalen Sieg beim Derby von 1924.

(Ci-dessus) La poésie en action. Steve Donoghue et Captain Cuttle remportent haut la main le Derby de 1922. (Ci-contre) La justice a le bras long. Sous la protection d'un policier en pèlerine, le 17ᵉ comte de Derby (qui porte un haut-de-forme) et Tommy Weston savourent le triomphe de Sansovino lors du Derby de 1924.

Success is sweet. Owner Jack Joel and his 1921 Derby winner Humorist, Steve Donoghue up. Humorist, one of the bravest horses ever, died a few weeks later from tuberculosis, on the day that the artist Sir Alfred Munnings had travelled down to sketch him at his Wantage stable.

Die süßen Früchte des Erfolgs. Jack Joel und sein siegreiches Pferd Humorist mit Jockey Steve Donoghue beim Derby von 1921. Humorist, eines der stattlichsten Pferde aller Zeiten, starb wenige Wochen später an Tuberkulose – just an dem Tag, als der Maler Sir Alfred Munnings Humorists Stall in Wantage aufsuchte, um das Pferd zu porträtieren.

Douce est la victoire. Le propriétaire Jack Joel et son cheval vainqueur Humorist, monté pas Steve Donoghue lors du Derby de 1921. Humorist, l'un des chevaux les plus courageux de tous les temps, devait succomber quelques semaines plus tard d'une tuberculose le jour même où l'artiste Sir Alfred Munnings se rendait l'écurie de Wantage pour le dessiner.

Captain courageous. Captain Cuttle strides through the top hats after winning the 1922 Derby. Captain Cuttle nearly did not run. He was lame in the preliminaries and quickly had to have a new shoe fitted.

Meinen Respekt, Herr Kapitän. Captain Cuttle segelt durch ein Meer von Zylindern nach seinem Derby-Sieg im Jahre 1922. Dabei wäre Captain Cuttle beinahe nicht angetreten: Im Vorlauf hinkte das Pferd noch und musste auf die Schnelle neu beschlagen werden.

Capitaine Courage. Après sa victoire dans le Derby de 1922, Captain Cuttle se fraie un chemin au milieu des hauts-de-forme. Boitant légèrement lors des éliminatoires, Captain Cuttle avait failli ne pas participer à la course et avait dû en toute urgence se faire poser un nouveau fer.

The longest journey. The 1923 Derby winner, Papyrus, arrives in the United States after travelling across the Atlantic on the SS *Aquitania*, October 1923. After his trip to America, Papyrus returned to Britain to run in the St Leger. Unsurprisingly, his exertions abroad told. Although he started as hot favourite, he was beaten by Tranquil.

Wenn einer eine Reise tut. Papyrus, frisch gebackener Derby-Sieger, bei seiner Ankunft in den Vereinigten Staaten im Oktober 1923. Hinter dem Pferd liegt eine Atlantiküberquerung auf der SS *Aquitania*. Im Anschluss an den Abstecher nach Übersee kehrte Papyrus nach Großbritannien zurück, um beim St. Leger zu starten. Wie zu erwarten, sollten sich die Strapazen bemerkbar machen. Zwar ging Papyrus als heißer Favorit ins Rennen, wurde aber von Tranquil geschlagen.

Un long voyage pour Papyrus, vainqueur du Derby en 1923, qui arrive aux États-Unis en octobre 1923 après avoir traversé l'Atlantique à bord du SS *Aquitania*. Suite à ce voyage, Papyrus revint en Grande-Bretagne pour participer au St-Leger. Évidemment, ses efforts outre-atlantique ne furent pas sans conséquences et, bien qu'étant parti grand favori, il dut laisser la victoire à Tranquil.

(Top, left) Grooms test the padded walls of Papyrus's stall on board. (Top, right) Bales of hay being carried onto the ship. (Above) Papyrus gets a motorcycle escort on his way to Belmont Park racecourse, New York, from the harbour.

(Oben links) Stallburschen überprüfen die gepolsterten Wände von Papyrus' „Bordkabine". (Oben rechts) Heuballen werden an Bord gebracht. (Oben) Eine Motorradeskorte bahnt Papyrus den Weg vom Hafen zur New Yorker Rennbahn Belmont Park.

(En haut, à gauche) À bord, les lads testent les parois capitonnées de la stalle destinée à Papyrus. (En haut, à droite) Transport des balles de foin à bord du bateau. (Ci-dessus) Papyrus est escorté de motards le long du trajet qui le mène du port au champ de courses de Belmont Park à New York.

Englishmen abroad. (Opposite) British jockey Charlie Smirke after winning the Grand Prix de Paris on Reine Lumière at Longchamp in June 1925. (Above) Steve Donoghue escorted by police and officials at Belmont Park before riding Papyrus. Papyrus failed to handle the soft ground conditions and was easily beaten in a match by the American champion, Zen.

Engländer im Ausland. (Gegenüber) Der britische Jockey Charlie Smirke auf Reine Lumière im Juni 1925 nach seinem Sieg beim Großen Preis von Paris in Longchamp. (Oben) Polizisten und Funktionäre begleiten Steve Donoghue vor seinem Ritt auf Papyrus zur Rennbahn von Belmont Park. Papyrus kam mit dem weichen Boden nicht zurecht und wurde vom amerikanischen Champion Zen mit Leichtigkeit abgehängt.

Des Anglais à l'étranger. (Ci-contre) Le jockey britannique Charlie Smirke après sa victoire obtenue en juin 1925 à Longchamp dans le Grand Prix de Paris sur Reine Lumière. (Ci-dessus) Steve Donoghue est escorté par la police et les officiels à Belmont Park avant de monter Papyrus qui, durant la course, ne parvint pas à se faire au terrain lourd et fut largement battu par le champion américain Zen.

Prologue and epilogue. (Above) An anxious moment for Steve Donoghue as his 1925 Derby mount Manna has the starting tape between his teeth. (Opposite) It made no difference: Manna produced the goods, coming home a well-backed 9/1 winner.

Vor- und Nachspiel. (Oben) Ein kritischer Augenblick für Steve Donoghue beim Derby von 1925 – sein Pferd Manna nimmt das Startband zwischen die Zähne. (Gegenüber) Es hat ihm nicht geschadet: Manna, auf das viele gesetzt hatten, ging als 9/1-Sieger durchs Ziel.

Prologue et épilogue. (Ci-dessus) Un moment de frayeur au départ du Derby de 1925 pour Steve Donoghue, dont le cheval Manna se retrouve avec le fil de départ entre les dents. (Ci-contre) Cela ne devait rien changer puisque Manna répondait aux espoirs placés en lui alors qu'il était coté à 9 contre un.

Fashion statements. (Above) A gypsy trader and two smartly dressed racegoers appear to be sharing a joke at Royal Ascot in June 1922. (Right) A lady in a striped dress haggles with a bookie on Oaks Day at Epsom in 1923.

Modische Bekenntnisse. (Oben) Ein Handel treibender Zigeuner und zwei elegant gekleidete Rennplatzbesucher scheinen beim Royal Ascot im Juni 1922 über einen gelungenen Witz zu lachen. (Rechts) Eine Lady im Streifenkleid feilscht mit einem Buchmacher am Oaks Day in Epsom, 1923.

Un défilé de mode. (Ci-dessus) Un commerçant gitan et deux amateurs de course tirés à quatre épingles semblent échanger des plaisanteries lors du Royal Ascot, juin 1922. (À droite) Marchandage à Epsom entre un bookmaker et une dame vêtue d'une robe à rayures, lors des Oaks Day d'Epsom, en 1923.

(Left) Bookmaker Steve Wall with a pile of betting tickets at Birmingham racecourse, November 1926. (Above) National dress and military uniforms can also be worn in Ascot's Royal Enclosure: a Scotsman places a bet at the 1923 Royal Meeting.

(Links) Der Buchmacher Steve Wall mit einem Stapel Wettscheine auf der Rennbahn von Birmingham im November 1926. (Oben) Auch Landestrachten und Militäruniformen waren im „königlichen" Publikumsbereich von Ascot erlaubt: Hier platziert ein Schotte seine Wette beim Royal Meeting von 1923.

(À gauche) Sur l'hippodrome de Birmingham, le bookmaker Steve Wall porte un tas de tickets de paris, novembre 1926. (Ci-dessus) Dans l'enceinte royale d'Ascot, les parures nationales et les uniformes militaires sont également de mise : ici, un Écossais place un pari lors du meeting royal d'Ascot, en 1923.

Thrills and spills (above and opposite) at Britain's jumping courses in the
Roaring Twenties. Clearly, falling head first through the front door is the least
elegant and most embarrassing way to part company with one's unfortunate
mount.

Spektakuläre Stürze (oben und gegenüber) auf den britischen Hindernis-
Strecken in den Goldenen Zwanzigern. Keine Frage: Kopfüber vom Pferd zu
fallen ist die uneleganteste und peinlichste Art, sich von seinem glücklosen
Vierbeiner zu trennen.

Des émotions et quelques bleus (Ci-dessus et ci-contre) durant les courses
d'obstacles des années folles. Abandonner son malheureux cheval en tombant
la tête la première vers l'avant manque définitivement d'élégance.

The meeting of two champions. After yet another awesome victory in 1920, the great American racehorse Man o' War, winner of twenty of his twenty-one starts, is admired by the heavyweight boxer Jack Dempsey (right). Trainer Louis Feustel stands on the left.

Stelldichein zweier Champions. Der Schwergewichtsboxer Jack Dempsey (rechts) bewundert das stolze amerikanische Rennpferd Man o' War nach einem weiteren atemberaubenden Sieg im Jahre 1920. Man o' War gewann 20 von 21 Rennen. Links im Bild: Trainer Louis Feustel.

La rencontre de deux champions. Après une nouvelle et époustouflante victoire en 1920, le superbe cheval de course américain Man o' War, vainqueur de 20 courses sur 21 participations, fait l'admiration du boxeur, catégorie poids lourds, Jack Dempsey, à droite. L'entraîneur Louis Feustel se tient sur la gauche.

Time to reflect. Man o' War's owner, Pennsylvania textile magnate Samuel D Riddle (left), and his trainer Louis Feustel, take a break from all the excitement at the training barn. Later, Man o' War might have been a more successful stallion if his owner had not restricted him to twenty-five mares a year.

Zeit zum Nachdenken. Man o' Wars Besitzer, der Textilmagnat Samuel D. Riddle aus Pennsylvania, und sein Trainer Louis Feustel gönnen sich vor dem Stall eine Pause von den Strapazen des Trainings. Vielleicht wäre Man o' War noch ein erfolgreicherer Zuchthengst geworden, wenn ihn sein Eigentümer nicht auf das Decken von 25 Stuten pro Jahr beschränkt hätte.

C'est l'heure de la réflexion pour Samuel D. Riddle, magnat du textile en Pennsylvanie et propriétaire de Man o' War, et son entraîneur Louis Feustel qui se remettent de leurs émotions à la porte de l'écurie. Par la suite, Man o' War aurait pu être un étalon plus prolifique mais son propriétaire le limitait à vingt-cinq saillies par an.

Look both ways before you cross. A policeman holds up passers-by as the runners cross the main road at the now defunct course at Chelmsford in Essex in 1928. On racecourses traversed by roads, turf or earth is laid on top of the tarmac to ensure horses have a safe surface to gallop over.

Vorsicht beim Überqueren der Straße. Ein Polizist hält Passanten auf, während die Teilnehmer der heute stillgelegten Rennstrecke Chelmsford in Essex die Hauptstraße überqueren, 1928. Kreuzt ein Straßen-abschnitt eine Rennstrecke, wird zum Schutz der Pferde Erdreich auf den Teer gebracht. Der Kurs in Chelmsford ist mittlerweile stillgelegt.

Regardez des deux côtés avant de traverser ! Un policier retient les passants au moment où les coureurs s'apprêtent à emprunter la route principale de l'hippodrome aujourd'hui disparu de Chelmsford, dans l'Essex, 1928. Lorsque les pistes des hippodromes sont traversées par des routes, le goudron est recouvert de terre ou de gazon pour permettre aux chevaux de passer en toute sécurité.

Divine guidance. The leaders clear a hurdle before
racing round St Michael's church on Galleywood
Common at the picturesque Chelmsford racecourse.

Himmlischer Beistand. Das Führungsduo überspringt
ein Hindernis, bevor es die pittoreske Rennstrecke von
Chelmsford bei Galleywood Common rund um die
St.-Michaels-Kirche führt.

Les voies du Seigneur. Les coureurs en tête franchissent
une haie avant de bifurquer devant l'église St-Michael,
sur le terrain communal de Galleywood où se trouve
l'hippodrome de Chelmsford.

The sublime and the ridiculous. (Opposite) The leader takes the water jump in style at Hawthorn Hill, a racecourse near Ascot popular with amateur, military riders, March 1929. (Above) Solomon and rider look destined for an early bath at the Old Surrey & Burstow point-to-point near Edenbridge, Kent, in April 1922.

Vollendung und Lächerlichkeit. (Gegenüber) Das in Führung liegende Pferd nimmt im März 1929 mit Bravour den Wassergraben von Hawthorn Hill, einer in der Nähe von Ascot liegenden, vor allem von Amateuren und Militäry-Reitern genutzten Strecke. (Oben) Pferd Solomon nebst Reiter auf dem Weg zu einem verfrühten Bad beim Geländejagdrennen Old Surrey & Burstow in der Nähe von Edenbridge, Kent, im April 1922.

Le sublime et le ridicule. (Ci-contre) C'est dans un style impeccable que le cheval de tête franchit la rivière d'Hawthorn Hill, un parcours près d'Ascot, utilisé surtout par des amateurs et des militaires, mars 1929. (Ci-dessus) Solomon et son cavalier semblent ne pas devoir échapper à un bain matinal lors de cette course d'obstacles en extérieur à Old Surrey & Burstow près d'Edenbridge, dans le Kent, avril 1922.

Father and son. Ted Leader returns on
Sprig, the winner of the 1927 Grand
National. Tom Leader, Sprig's trainer, was
the proud father of the successful jockey.
Tom Leader also saddled another National
winner, Gregalach, and Ted became a
competent Newmarket flat trainer.

Vater und Sohn. Ted Leader auf Sprig nach
ihrem Sieg in der Grand National von 1927.
Sprigs Trainer Tom Leader war zugleich
stolzer Vater des erfolgreichen Jockeys.
Er trainierte mit Gregalach noch einen
weiteren National-Gewinner. Sohn Ted
arbeitete später als gefragter Flachrennen-
Trainer in Newmarket.

Le père et le fils. Ted Leader triomphe avec
Sprig, le vainqueur du Grand National de
1927. Tom Leader, l'entraîneur de Sprig,
était aussi l'heureux père du jeune jockey.
Tom Leader fit également courir Gregalach,
un autre vainqueur du Grand National, et
son fils Ted devint un entraîneur talentueux
sur le plat, à Newmarket.

Studying the form. Three Parisian punters pose in front of the Tote odds board at Longchamp in 1925. Hats were always worn by men in the smarter enclosures on European racecourses in the pre-war years.

Formstudien. Drei Wettfreunde aus Paris posieren vor der Totalisator-Anzeige des Rennens in Longchamp, 1925. Für das männliche Publikum war es auf europäischen Rennbahnen in den Jahren vor dem Krieg ein Muss, Hüte zu tragen.

Étudier les performances. À Longchamp, en 1925, trois parieurs parisiens posent devant le tableau des cotes de Tote. Sur les plus élégants hippodromes d'Europe, durant les années précédant la guerre, les hommes portaient toujours un chapeau.

Lucky winners. French gamblers queue to collect their winnings at the
10 franc windows of the Julius Tote at Longchamp, on Arc de Triomphe Day,
1925. Clearly they have backed the winner, Priori, trained by Percy Carter.

Glückliche Gewinner. Französische Glücksspieler in Longchamp stehen am
Arc-de-Triomphe-Tag des Jahres 1925 an den 10-Francs-Schaltern Schlange,
um ihren Gewinn beim Totalisator einzulösen. Offensichtlich hatten sie auf
den Sieger Priori, trainiert von Percy Carter, gesetzt.

Heureux gagnants. Sur l'hippodrome de Longchamp, le jour du Grand Prix de
l'Arc de Triomphe de 1925, les parieurs français font la queue aux guichets à
10F de Julius Tote pour encaisser leurs gains. Ils avaient évidemment misé sur
Priori, le vainqueur, entraîné par Percy Carter.

It's good to talk. (Above, left) Royal trainer, Cecil Boyd-Rochfort, and Lady Grimthorpe at York, 25 August 1927. (Above, right) Trainers Stanley Wootton (on crutches) and Harry Escott at Hurst Park, 2 May 1925. (Opposite) Miss Monica Sheriffe and Mrs James Seely at the Quorn Hunt point-to-point meeting at Loughborough, 23 April 1929.

Ein gutes Gespräch. (Oben links) Der königliche Trainer Cecil Boyd-Rochfort und Lady Grimthorpe in York, 25. August 1927. (Oben rechts) Die Trainer Stanley Wootton (auf Krücken) und Harry Escott im Hurst Park am 2. Mai 1925. (Gegenüber) Miss Monica Sheriffe und Mrs. James Seely bei der Quorn-Hunt-Geländejagd in Loughborough am 23. April 1929.

Un brin de causette. (Ci-dessus à gauche) Cecil Boyd-Rochfort, entraîneur pour le compte de la famille royale, en compagnie de Lady Grimthorpe, à York, le 25 août 1927. (Ci-dessus, à droite) Les entraîneurs Stanley Wootton (avec des béquilles) et Harry Escott à Hurst Park, le 2 mai 1925. (Ci-contre) Mlle Monica Sheriffe et Mme James Seely discutent lors de la course d'obstacles de Quorn Hunt à Loughborough, le 23 avril 1929.

Fashion exclusive. Photographer Leslie Henson towers above all others as he uses the latest box camera to snap the glitterati on Tuesday 17 June 1924, the first day of the Royal Ascot meeting. Shiny black silk top hats, rather than grey ones, were the correct headgear in those halcyon times.

Exklusive Mode. Der Fotograf Leslie Henson lichtet die Schickeria ab und ragt dabei mit seiner nagelneuen Boxkamera aus der Menge heraus. Das Bild entstand am Dienstag, den 17. Juni 1924, dem ersten Tag des Royal Ascot Meetings. In diesen unbeschwerten Tagen trug man(n) übrigens glänzende schwarze anstelle von grauen Seidenzylindern.

Une exclusivité. Le photographe Leslie Henson domine l'assemblée tandis qu'il teste le tout dernier modèle d'appareil photo pour prendre des clichés de célébrités présentes ce mardi 17 juin 1924, premier jour du Royal Ascot. En cette heureuse période, les couvre-chefs en soie noire brillante étaient plus en vogue que ceux de couleur grise.

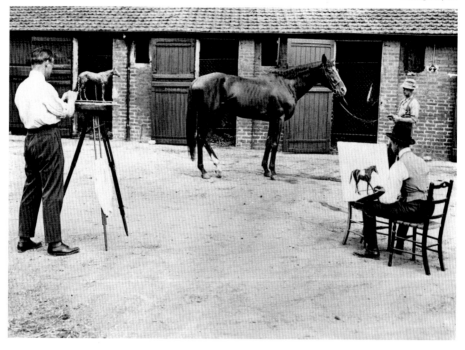

Artistic licence. An artist and a sculptor attempt to capture the likeness of the famous French horse Epinard in 1924. Epinard made several successful cross-Channel raids on big British prizes and landed an enormous gamble when he won the Stewards' Cup at Goodwood in 1923.

Still stehen für die Kunst. Ein Maler und ein Bildhauer beim Versuch, das berühmte französische Rennpferd Epinard möglichst naturgetreu wiederzugeben, 1924. Epinard startete mehrfach in Großbritannien und siegte dort bei großen Preisen. Beim Stewards' Cup von 1923 in Goodwood erzielte das Pferd gigantische Quoten.

Une licence artistique. En 1924, un dessinateur et un peintre tentent de représenter Epinard, le célèbre cheval français. Epinard s'est rendu plusieurs fois outre-Manche pour s'y imposer lors d'importantes épreuves et réussit même le fabuleux pari de remporter la Steward's Cup à Goodwood en 1923.

The American dream. Owner W R Coe greets his two-year-old Pompey and jockey L Fator after a victory in the $75,000 Futurity at Belmont Park, Long Island. Fator is riding shorter than most European jockeys did at the time.

Der amerikanische Traum. Pferdebesitzer W. R. Coe präsentiert den Zweijährigen Pompey mit Jockey L. Fator nach ihrem Sieg im mit 75 000 US Dollar dotierten Futurity in Belmont Park, Long Island. Fator reitet in kürzeren Steigriemen, als es in Europa zu jener Zeit üblich war.

Le rêve américain. W. R. Coe, propriétaire de Pompey, félicite son cheval ainsi que le jockey L. Fator après leur victoire lors du Futurity, doté d'un prix de 75 000$ et couru à Belmont Park, dans l'État de Long Island. Fator monte plus court que la plupart des jockeys européens à la même époque.

Top American jockey Albert Johnson gets a congratulatory hug from the winning owner after Exterminator's victory at Aqueduct, the famous American racecourse, on 16 June 1922.

Der amerikanische Top-Jockey Albert Johnson wird vom Besitzer des siegreichen Pferdes beglückwünscht. Johnson gewann am 16. Juni 1922 mit Exterminator auf der berühmten amerikanischen Aqueduct-Rennbahn.

Albert Johnson, le brillant jockey américain, reçoit les félicitations du propriétaire d'Exterminator, qui vient d'emporter la course sur le célèbre hippodrome américain d'Aqueduct, 16 juin 1922.

April showers. A sea of umbrellas as the runners in the Great Metropolitan Handicap head up the hill at the Epsom Spring Meeting 1926. The Great Metropolitan was the longest race run at Epsom. The competitors even left the racecourse proper for a time to wend their way around the Downs.

Aprilwetter. Eingerahmt von Regenschirmen nehmen die Teilnehmer den Hügel des Great Metropolitan Handicap beim 1926er Frühjahrsmeeting in Epsom. The Great Metropolitan war das längste Rennen von Epsom. Manchmal verließen die Reiter sogar kurzerhand den Kurs, um sich an den Steigungen vorbeizumogeln.

Averses d'avril. Réunion de printemps à Epsom. Le public s'abrite sous un océan de parapluies tandis que les participants au handicap du Great Metropolitan gravissent la côte, 1926. Le Great Metropolitan était l'épreuve la plus longue courue à Epsom. Le parcours les amenait même à quitter l'hippodrome proprement dit pour poursuivre leur route dans les Downs.

Autumn rains. Cyril Ray (left) and Jackie Sirett protect themselves from a deluge at Worcester in October 1926. Ray had the unenviable distinction of being warened off as a jockey and as a trainer.

Herbstregen. Cyril Ray (links) und Jackie Sirett schützen sich vor einem Guss in Worcester, Oktober 1926. Ray vollbrachte das wenig beneidenswerte Kunststück als Jockey wie als Trainer unrühmlich entlassen zu werden.

Pluies d'automne. En ce jour d'octobre 1926, Cyril Ray (à gauche) et Jackie Sirett se protègent des trombes d'eau qui s'abattent sur Worcester. Ray pouvait se prévaloir d'une distinction peu enviable, puisqu'il était exclu en tant que jockey qu'en tant qu'entraîneur.

Three of a kind. A trio of leading riders of the 1928 flat season. Left to right, Harry Wragg, Gordon Richards and Freddie Fox have a smile for the camera at one of the year's last meetings at the now closed Alexandra Park track in London, 3 November 1928.

Drei Artverwandte. Dieses Trio dominierte die Flachrennen der Saison 1928. Es sind, von links nach rechts, Harry Wragg, Gordon Richards und Freddie Fox, die hier bei einem der letzten Rennen des Jahres auf der mittlerweile geschlossenen Alexandra-Park-Rennbahn in London in die Kamera lächeln, 3. November 1928.

Trois d'une même espèce. Ce trio domina la saison des épreuves sur plat dans la saison 1928. De gauche à droite : Harry Wragg, Gordon Richards et Freddie Fox sourient sur la photographie prise le 3 novembre 1928, lors de l'un des derniers meetings de l'année à l'Alexandra Park de Londres, aujourd'hui fermé.

Darling of the Turf.
The famous Beck-
hampton trainer
Fred Darling
discusses a race with
jockey Joe Childs in
1926. Darling, who
was a martinet,
insisted that jockeys
obeyed his instruc-
tions to the letter.

Darling des Turfs.
Fred Darling, ruhm-
reicher Trainer des
Beckhampton-Stalls,
und Jockey Joe
Childs bei der Be-
sprechung eines
Rennens von 1926.
Der als „harter
Hund" bekannte
Darling bestand
darauf, dass die
Jockeys seine An-
weisungen peinlich
genau befolgten.

La coqueluche des
hippodromes. Le
célèbre entraîneur
de Beckhampton,
Fred Darling, discute
d'une course avec le
jockey Joe Childs,
1926. Darling, très
à cheval sur la disci-
pline, tenait à ce
que les jockeys
suivent à la lettre
ses instructions.

Dish of the day. Harry Wragg, who was known as the 'Head Waiter', because he liked to bring his mounts with a late winning run, returning after taking the 1928 Derby on Felstead. At a time when it was thought necessary to lead for most of the way to win the Derby, Wragg flew in the face of convention by evolving successful waiting tactics on Felstead.

Tagesgericht. Jockey Harry Wraggs Eigenart, stets aus der zweiten Reihe zum Schluss-Sprint anzusetzen, trug ihm den Spitznamen „der Oberkellner" ein. Hier wird Wragg nach seinem Derby-Sieg von 1928 auf Felstead zum Stall geführt. Damals glaubte man, die meiste Zeit in Führung liegen zu müssen, um das Derby zu gewinnen. Wragg scherte sich nicht um die Konventionen und perfektionierte mit Felstead eine erfolgreiche Lauer-Taktik.

Le plat du jour. Harry Wragg, dont l'habitude de remporter les courses à l'issue d'un sprint final lui avait valu le surnom de « maître d'hôtel », rentre après sa victoire dans le Derby de 1928 sur Felstead. À cette époque, on estimait que, pour remporter le Derby, il était nécessaire de disputer la majeure partie de la course en tête. Avec Felstead, Wragg prouvait le contraire en adoptant une tactique de dernière minute qui se révéla payante.

Perfect timing. Wragg brings Felstead to the front at the opportune moment to score easily by one and a half lengths from Flamingo. Wragg had the rare distinction of both riding and training a Derby winner. He won three Derbys as a jockey and saddled Psidium to take the 1961 race.

Perfektes Timing. In einem günstigen Moment zieht Felstead an Flamingo vorbei und siegt um komfortable anderthalb Längen. Wragg gelang das überaus seltene Kunststück, das Derby dreimal als Jockey und später auch einmal als Trainer (1961 mit Psidium) zu gewinnen.

Le bon moment. Wragg prend les commandes avec Felstead au moment opportun pour l'emporter facilement, avec une longueur et demie d'avance sur Flamingo. Wragg réussit l'exploit assez rare de gagner le Derby à la fois en tant qu'entraîneur et jockey. Il remporta en effet cette épreuve trois fois en tant que jockey et fut aussi l'entraîneur de Psidium, vainqueur de l'édition en 1961.

German glory days. The golden age of German racing between the wars. Horses are led out for the Hindenburg race at Berlin. Many British jockeys and trainers plied their trade in Germany in the early years of the century, including the legendary trainer Fred Darling.

Der deutsche Pferderennsport erlebte zwischen den Weltkriegen sein goldenens Zeitalter. Hier werden die Pferde in Berlin für den Hindenburg-Pokal herausgeführt. Zahlreiche britische Jockeys und Trainer arbeiteten im frühen 20. Jahrhundert in Deutschland, darunter der legendäre Trainer Fred Darling.

L'époque glorieuse de l'Allemagne. L'âge d'or des courses en Allemagne se situe durant l'entre-deux-guerres. Les chevaux sont conduits sur le terrain de course berlinois où ils vont disputer le Prix Hindenburg. Au début du siècle, de nombreux jockeys et entraîneurs britanniques exerçaient leur métier en Allemagne, dont le légendaire Fred Darling.

Ammaisch returns to
the unsaddling
enclosure with an
anxious policeman
after winning the
prestigious German
Derby at Hamburg
in July 1924.

Ein dienststeifriger
Polizist begleitet
Ammaisch auf dem
Weg zum Absatteln
nach seinem Sieg im
Deutschen Derby
von Hamburg im
Juli 1924.

Ammaisch retourne
au paddock pour y
être dessellé sous
l'œil inquiet d'un
policier après sa
victoire dans le
prestigieux Derby
allemand couru à
Hambourg en
juillet 1924.

Packed to the rafters. Derby Day at
Epsom in June 1927. Vast crowds
attended the Derby between the
wars. Every blade of grass on the
Downs seemed to be covered with a
colourful mass of spectators keen to
have a flutter on the world's most
famous horse race.

Großer Andrang beim Derby Day,
Epsom, im Juni 1927. Zwischen den
Kriegen zog das Derby enorme
Zuschauermengen an. Bis in die
letzten Winkel des Geländes rund um
die Rennstrecke drängte sich die bunt
gemischte Zuschauermenge, die das
große Glück beim berühmtesten
Galopprennen der Welt suchte.

Serrés comme des sardines. Jour de
Derby à Epsom en juin 1927. Durant
l'entre-deux-guerres, une foule
considérable y assistait. Toute la
superficie des Downs était occupée
par une foule bigarrée, avide de parier
à l'occasion d'une course considérée
comme la plus célèbre au monde.

(Above) Amateur jockey Jack Anthony, who rode
three Grand National winners, with a lady
admirer at Wincanton, Somerset, October 1925.
(Left) Bussed to the races. Open-topped buses line
the course on Derby Day.

(Oben) Der Amateur-Jockey und dreifache Grand-
National-Sieger Jack Anthony mit einer Verehrerin
in Wincanton, Somerset, Oktober 1925.
(Links) Mit dem Bus zum Rennen. Doppeldecker-
Busse mit offenem Verdeck säumen die Rennbahn
am Derby Day.

(Ci-dessus) Le jockey amateur Jack Anthony, trois
fois vainqueur du Grand National, avec une admira-
trice à Wincanton, dans le Somerset, octobre 1925.
(À gauche) Terminus : les courses. Le jour du Derby,
les autobus à impériale bordent l'hippodrome.

The exuberance of youth. Norah Wilmot, one of the first lady
trainers, lunges a yearling colt by the Derby winner Spion Kop.
Miss Wilmot trained many winners at her stables at Binfield, near Ascot.

Ungestüme Jugend. Norah Wilmot, eine der ersten weiblichen
Trainer, longiert ein einjähriges Fohlen des Derby-Siegers Spion Kop.
Aus Miss Wilmots Stall in Binfield nahe Ascot gingen viele siegreiche
Pferde hervor.

La fougue de la jeunesse. Norah Wilmot, l'une des toutes premières
entraîneuses, travaille à la longe avec ce jeune cheval, aux côtes du
vainqueur du Derby, Spion Kop. Mlle Wilmot a entraîné de nombreux
vainqueurs dans ses écuries de Binfield, près d'Ascot.

The speed of light. Mumtaz Mahal, known as 'the Flying Filly', after winning
the Champagne Stakes at Doncaster in 1923. George Hulme is the rider of the
two-year-old filly whose sire was The Tetrarch, another speedy grey.

Mit Lichtgeschwindigkeit. Jockey George Hulme mit Mumtaz Mahal, bekannt als „das
fliegende Fohlen", nach ihrem Sieg in den Champagne Stakes von Doncaster im Jahre
1923. Der Zuchthengst des zweijährigen Füllens war der ebenfalls rasante Schimmel
The Tetrarch.

À la vitesse de la lumière. Mumtaz Mahal, connue sous le nom de « la pouliche volante »
après sa victoire dans le Prix Champagne de Doncaster, en 1923. La pouliche, âgée de
deux ans, est montée par George Hulme. Son géniteur n'était autre que The Tetrarch
dont elle a hérité de la robe grise et de la vélocité légendaire.

(Above) Any chance of a lift home? Two jockeys return in tandem after the Grand National when only two runners completed the course, 30 March 1928. (Left) The winner, Tipperary Tim, and jockey Bill Dutton. Few punters backed Tipperary Tim, who started at 100/1.

(Oben) Huckepack nach Hause. Zwei Jockeys kehren im Tandem von der Grand National am 30. März 1928 zurück. In jenem Jahr erreichten nur zwei Pferde das Ziel. (Links) Sieger Tipperary Tim mit Jockey Bill Dutton. Das Pferd, auf das nur wenige setzten, ging mit der Quote 100/1 ins Rennen.

(Ci-dessus) Vous me déposez à la maison? Retour groupé de deux jockeys à la fin du Grand National couru le 30 mars 1928. Deux concurrents seulement avaient réussi à terminer la course. (À gauche) Le vainqueur, Tipperary Tim et son jockey Bill Dutton. Peu de parieurs avaient misé sur Tipperary Tim qui affichait au départ une cote de 100 contre 1.

Hindquarters. The leader shows the rest of the field a clean pair of heels in the first race at a 1926 Newmarket fixture. Newmarket's flat heathland is the home of two racecourses, the Rowley Mile and the July Courses, and numerous training stables. The Suffolk town has been the headquarters of British racing since Charles II's time.

Im Hintertreffen. Das führende Pferd hängt seine Verfolger im ersten Rennen der Newmarket-Konkurrenz von 1926 locker ab. Das flache Heideland von Newmarket beherbergt mit Rowley Mile und July zwei Rennstrecken sowie zahlreiche Trainingsställe. Seit der Zeit Charles II. galt die Stadt in Suffolk als Zentrum des britischen Pferderennens.

Filer le train. Le cheval de tête ne laisse voir que ses sabots aux autres concurrents durant la première course disputée lors d'une rencontre à Newmarket en 1926. Les landes plates de Newmarket où se disputent deux épreuves, le Rowley Mile et les Courses de Juillet, abritent de nombreuses écuries d'entraînement. Depuis l'époque de Charles II, la ville du Suffolk est le quartier général du monde des courses britanniques.

I spy with my little eye. On the roof of a taxi an enterprising racegoer uses his female companion's head as a telescope rest to watch the 1921 Derby.

Der Spion, der mich liebte. Dieser kühne Rennplatzbesucher macht den Kopf seiner Gefährtin kurzerhand zur Auflage für sein Fernrohr. Beide verfolgen das 1921er Derby vom Dach eines Taxis.

Par le petit bout de la lorgnette. Cet amateur de courses ne manque pas d'initiative et utilise la tête de sa compagne pour suivre sur le toit d'un taxi le Derby de 1921.

Packed in like sardines, French racegoers appear to be risking their lives for a good view of the sport on a rickety, improvised wooden grandstand at Nice racecourse, January 1920. Nice racecourse closed when the city's modern airport was built. Riviera racing now takes place at Cagnes-sur-Mer further down the coast.

Dicht gedrängt wie Sardinen riskieren die französischen Zuschauer auf der wackligen improvisierten Tribüne der Rennbahn von Nizza für einen guten Ausblick ihr Leben, Januar 1920. Später musste die Bahn dem neuen Flughafen der Stadt weichen und das Renngeschehen der Riviera verlagerte sich die Küste hinab nach Cagnes-sur-Mer.

Nice, janvier 1920. Serrés comme des sardines, ces turfistes français semblent ne pas hésiter à risquer leurs vies pour pouvoir mieux suivre la course du haut d'une tribune en bois improvisée et visiblement peu fiable. L'hippodrome de Nice devait fermer avec la construction de l'aéroport moderne. Aujourd'hui, les courses sur la Côte d'Azur se déroulent à Cagnes-sur-Mer, plus à l'ouest sur la côte.

A grand design. Balderston wins the Banstead Plate at Epsom in April 1927. The steep descent of the course from Tattenham Corner is clearly visible in the background. Epsom's new grandstand on the left of the picture was first used at the 1927 Spring Meeting.

Ein großer Wurf. Balderston gewinnt die Banstead Plate von Epsom im April 1927. Im Hintergrund deutlich zu erkennen: das steile Gefälle der Rennstrecke nach der Tattenham-Kurve. Links im Bild die neue Haupttribüne, die in jenem Frühjahr eingeweiht worden war.

Une construction imposante. Balderston remporte le Bandstead Plate d'Epsom en avril 1927. En arrière-plan, on voit nettement la descente prononcée depuis le virage de Tattenham. À gauche de la photographie, la nouvelle tribune d'Epsom, inaugurée lors de la réunion de printemps de la même année.

3. Halcyon days
Glückliche Tage
Les jours heureux

Too much winning takes the fun away. Owner Marcel Boussac and jockey Charlie Elliott look pensive after winning yet another big race, the 1939 Grand Prix de Paris at Longchamp, with Pharis II. The famous tipster 'Prince' Raz Monolulu, whose regular catchphrase was 'I got a horse', can be seen in the plumed headgear.

Zu viele Siege verderben die Freude. Trotz eines weiteren großen Triumphs im 1939er Grand Prix de Paris in Longchamp blicken Jockey Charlie Elliott mit Pharis II. und Besitzer Marcel Boussac eher nachdenklich drein. Der gefiederte Kopfputz gehört zu dem bekannten Tippgeber „Prinz" Raz Monolulu, dessen Lieblings-Ausspruch „I got a horse" („Ich habe da ein Pferd...") in die Geschichte einging.

Trop de victoires gâchent le plaisir. Le propriétaire Marcel Boussac et le jockey Charlie Elliott semblent plongés dans leurs pensées après une nouvelle victoire dans une grande course : Pharis vient d'emporter l'édition de 1939 du Grand Prix de Paris, à Longchamp. Le célèbre pronostiqueur « Prince » Raz Monolulu, qui avait coutume d'annoncer « j'ai un bon cheval », apparaît à l'arrière-plan, coiffé de plumes.

The Thirties was a decade for breaking records: Gordon Richards rode 259 winners in 1933; Golden Miller won five Cheltenham Gold Cups in a row; Brown Jack, the public's favourite, took Royal Ascot's Queen Alexandra Stakes for six successive years. At seventeen, Bruce Hobbs became both the youngest and the tallest jockey to win the Grand National, on Battleship, still the smallest horse to triumph in steeplechasing's greatest test. Another diminutive mount, Hyperion, proved that size is not everything, taking the 1933 Derby and St Leger. Two years later Bahram joined an exclusive club of Triple Crown winners when he won the 2,000 Guineas, the Derby and the St Leger for the Aga Khan. In France the textile magnate Marcel Boussac laid the foundations for one of the greatest racing and breeding empires ever to have existed in Europe. Federico Tesio also put Italian racing on the international map. He bred and trained Nearco, who beat the English and French Derby winners in the 1938 Grand Prix de Paris. And on the other side of the world, Phar Lap, the most famous racehorse ever born in the Southern Hemisphere, took Australian racing by storm, landing a host of big prizes in the early Thirties.

Die dreißiger Jahre waren das Jahrzehnt der Rekorde: Gordon Richards ritt 1933 zu sage und schreibe 259 Siegen, Golden Miller holte den Cheltenham Gold Cup fünf Mal in Folge und Publikumsliebling Brown Jack konnte die Queen Alexandra Stakes von Royal Ascot gar in sechs aufeinander folgenden Jahren für sich entscheiden. Mit 17 Jahren wurde Bruce Hobbs zum jüngsten und gleichzeitig körperlich größten Jockey, der je die Grand National gewann – auf Battleship, dem bis heute kleinsten Pferd, das diesen weltweit schwersten Hindernislauf als Sieger beendete. Dass Größe nicht alles ist, stellte mit Hyperion noch ein weiterer „Winzling" unter Beweis, der 1933 sowohl das Derby als auch das St. Leger gewann. Zwei Jahre darauf erweiterte Bahram – das Pferd des Aga Khan – den exklusiven Kreis von Triple-Crown-Siegern, als es die 2 000 Guineas, das Derby und das Rennen von St. Leger für seinen Besitzer gewinnen konnte. In Frankreich legte derweil der Textilmagnat Marcel Boussac den Grundstein für eines der größten Zucht- und Renn-Imperien in der Geschichte des europäischen Pferdesports. Federico Tesio hingegen führte den italienischen Pferderennsport zu internationalem Ruhm: Er züchtete und trainierte das Pferd Nearco, das die Derby-Sieger Frankreichs und Englands beim Grand Prix von Paris des Jahres 1938 hinter sich ließ. Auf der Südhalbkugel eroberte Phar Lap den australischen Rennsport im Sturm. Das berühmteste Rennpferd, das jemals in der südlichen Hemisphäre zur Welt kam, gewann in den frühen Dreißigern gleich eine ganze Reihe großer Preise.

Les années trente furent la décennie de tous les records. En 1933, Gordon Richards remportait la bagatelle de 259 courses. Golden Miller s'adjugeait cinq fois consécutives la Cheltenham Gold Cup tandis que Brown Jack, la coqueluche du public, enlevait le Prix Queen Alexandra du Royal Ascot durant six années consécutives. À 17 ans, Bruce Hobbs devint à la fois le plus jeune et le plus grand jockey à remporter le Grand National sur Battleship, qui reste encore le plus petit cheval à avoir gagné l'épreuve reine du steeple-chase. Hyperion, un autre de « petit format », apporta la preuve que la taille ne fait pas tout en remportant le Derby de 1933 et le Prix de St Leger. Deux ans plus tard, Bahram rejoignait le club très fermé des montures ayant remporté trois titres en s'adjugeant les 2 000 Guinées, le Derby et le Prix de St Leger pour le compte de l'Aga Khan. En France, Marcel Boussac, le roi du textile, fondait l'un des plus fabuleux empires ayant jamais existé en Europe dans le domaine des courses et de l'élevage. Federico Tesio, éleveur et entraîneur de Nearco qui, lors du Grand Prix de Paris de 1938, s'imposait face aux vainqueurs français et anglais du Derby, propulsait les montures italiennes au niveau international. À l'autre bout de la planète, Phar Lap révolutionnait le monde des courses australiennes et s'imposait comme le meilleur cheval de course de tous les temps dans l'hémisphère Sud en remportant de nombreux titres de premier plan au début des années trente.

As long as a piece of string. A string of racehorses trained by Frank Butters crosses Newmarket Heath during a morning exercise, 10 October 1931. Butters, who prepared the Derby winners Mahmoud and Bahram, was one of Britain's most successful trainers, winning fifteen Classics between 1928 and 1948.

Wie auf einer Schnur aufgereiht. Rennpferde beim morgendlichen Training in der Heide von Newmarket unter der Leitung von Frank Butters, 10. Oktober 1931. Butters, der die Derby-Sieger Mahmoud und Bahram trainiert hatte, war einer der erfolgreichsten Trainer Großbritanniens. Zwischen 1928 und 1948 gewann er 15 klassische Rennen.

Une longue file. Colonne de chevaux entraînés par Frank Butters, traversant les landes de Newmarket durant l'exercice matinal, 10 octobre 1931. Butters s'est chargé de la préparation de Mahmoud et Bahram, vainqueurs du Derby, était l'un des entraîneurs britanniques les plus capés, remportant quinze classiques entre 1928 et 1948.

Spring fever. Steve Donoghue on Marathon Man, an early season winner at Lincoln, 19 March 1934. Lincoln racecourse, which closed in 1964, always hosted the start of the flat season. The feature race was the Lincoln Handicap which, coupled with the Grand National, was the second leg of the then popular bet, 'the Spring Double'.

Frühlingsgefühle. Steve Donoghue und Marathon Man verbuchen zu Beginn der Saison den Sieg in Lincoln, 19. März 1934. Die 1964 stillgelegte Lincoln-Rennbahn eröffnete traditionell die Saison der Flach-rennen. Das Hauptrennen, das Lincoln Handicap, bildete gemeinsam mit der Grand National die beliebte Spring-Double-Wette.

Fièvre printanière. Steve Donoghue montant Marathon Man, vainqueur à Lincoln en ce début de saison. L'hippodrome de Lincoln, fermé en 1964, marquait traditionnellement le début de la saison des courses de plat, 19 mars 1934. La course, appelée le handi-cap Lincoln, était couplée avec le Grand National pour constituer la seconde manche d'un pari alors populaire, le « Spring Double » (Doublé du Printemps).

A royal procession. The Duke and Duchess of York, later to become King George VI and Queen Elizabeth, arrive by carriage at Royal Ascot, 16 June 1931. The royal procession of landaus which brings the monarch's party down the racecourse on each day of Royal Ascot, is one of British racing's great traditional spectacles.

Königliche Prozession. Der Herzog und die Herzogin von York (später König Georg VI. und Königin Elizabeth) bei ihrer Ankunft mit der Kutsche in Royal Ascot am 16. Juni 1931. Die traditionelle Kutschenprozession, die den königlichen Tross an jedem Royal-Ascot-Tag zur Rennbahn bringt, gehört zu den großen Ereignissen des britischen Pferderennens.

Une procession royale. Arrivée en carrosse au Royal Ascot du duc et de la duchesse de York, qui allaient devenir le roi George VI et la reine Elizabeth, 16 juin 1931. La procession royale des landaus conduisant la famille royale sur les hippodromes est l'un des grands spectacles dans la plus pure tradition des courses britanniques.

A royal wave.
Leading owner, the
Aga Khan III, head
of the Ismaili sect of
Shia Muslims, and
his wife, the Begum,
acknowledge friends.

Hoheitliches Winken.
Aga Khan III. –
Pferdemogul und
Oberhaupt der mus-
limischen Ismail-
Religionsgemein-
schaft – und seine
Frau, die Begum,
begrüßen Freunde.

Un salut royal. Le
plus important pro-
priétaire de chevaux,
l'Aga Khan III, chef
de la secte d'Ismaili
et des musulmans
Shia, et son épouse
la Begum saluent
des amis.

(Previous pages)
The Aga Khan's
Mahmoud and
Charlie Smirke
take the Derby,
27 May 1936 and
are led in by a
delighted Aga Khan
(left). Mahmoud
broke the Epsom
track record, helped
by the firm ground.

(Vorherige Doppel-
seite) Aga Khans
Mahmoud und
Charlie Smirke
holen sich das Derby
und werden von
einem sichtlich zu-
friedenen Aga Khan
von der Bahn ge-
führt (links),
27. Mai 1936. Be-
günstigt vom festen
Geläuf, stellte
Mahmoud einen
neuen Strecken-
rekord in Epsom auf.

(Pages précédentes)
Mahmoud, le cheval
de l'Aga Khan monté
par Charlie Smirke,
remporte le Derby
ce 27 mai 1936.
Il est conduit par
Aga Khan, visible-
ment ravi (à gauche).
Mahmoud, aidé par
un terrain ferme,
vient de battre le
record de la piste
d'Epsom.

Flying Fox. Freddie Fox takes the 1935 Triple Crown winner, Bahram, to post. In 1940 the Aga Khan sold Bahram to a syndicate of American breeders for £40,000. The sale caused resentment among British stud owners who were furious at losing a potential champion sire.

Freddie Fox auf der Zielgeraden mit dem 1935er Triple-Crown-Sieger Bahram. 1940 verkaufte der Aga Khan das Pferd für 40 000 Pfund an eine amerikanische Stallgemeinschaft und zog damit den Zorn britischer Gestüte auf sich, die den Verlust eines aussichtsreichen Zuchthengstes beklagten.

Freddie Fox s'envole vers le poteau d'arrivée pour cette troisième couronne de Bahram en 1935. En 1940, l'Aga Khan a vendu Bahram à un consortium d'éleveurs américains pour 40 000£. Cette vente suscita la réprobation des propriétaires de haras britanniques, furieux de voir partir un reproducteur potentiel de champions.

The Miller's Tale. (Above) Evan Williams and Golden Miller on the way to a record fifth consecutive Cheltenham Gold Cup triumph, 12 March 1936. (Left) Golden Miller at exercise on trainer Owen Anthony's gallops at Letcombe Bassett, Oxfordshire, 9 November 1936.

Die Miller-Legende. (Oben) Evan Williams mit Golden Miller auf ihrem Weg zum Rekord: dem fünften Cheltenham-Gold-Cup-Sieg in Folge am 12. März 1936. (Links) Golden Miller beim Training auf Owen Anthonys Gelände in Letcombe Bassett, Oxfordshire, 9. November 1936.

La légende de Miller. (Ci-dessus) Evan Williams et Golden Miller sont en route pour un record, avec cette cinquième victoire consécutive dans la Gold Cup de Cheltenham, le 12 mars 1936. (À gauche) Un peu d'exercice pour Golden Miller, monté par son entraîneur Owen Anthony à Letcombe Bassett, dans l'Oxfordshire, 9 novembre 1936.

A day at the seaside. Racehorses trained by David Dale are silhouetted against the Channel skyline as they walk along the beach at Newhaven in Sussex, 14 February 1938. The triple Grand National winner Red Rum was also trained on sand. All his exercise was conducted on Southport beach in Lancashire.

Ein Tag am Meer. Die Silhouetten einiger von David Dale trainierter Rennpferde im Gegenlicht am Ufer des Ärmelkanals am Strand von Newhaven, Sussex, 14. Februar 1938. Ebenfalls auf Sand – am Strand von Southport in Lancashire – wurde der dreifache Grand-National-Sieger Red Rum trainiert.

Bord de mer. Les silhouettes des chevaux entraînés par David Dale se découpent sur l'horizon de la Manche à Newhaven, dans le Sussex, 14 février 1938. C'est aussi sur des terrains sablonneux, sur la plage de Southport, dans le Lancashire, que s'entraînait Red Rum, trois fois vainqueur du Grand National.

Sandy shore. The Boy in Blue and his stable lad take an early morning gallop on the sands at Bognor Regis, Dorset, 13 February 1936. Before the invention of the artificial, all-weather gallop, many trainers took their horses to the beach when their grass working grounds were frozen.

Sandstrand. The Boy in Blue und sein Stallbursche beim morgendlichen Galopp am Strand von Bognor Regis, Dorset, 13. Februar 1936. Vor Einführung des künstlichen Galopperbodens wichen viele Trainer auf Sand aus, wenn der heimische Trainingsboden gefroren war.

Rivage de sable. The Boy in Blue est monté par son garçon d'écurie pour un galop matinal sur la plage de Bognor Regis, Dorset, 13 février 1936. Avant l'invention des terrains artificiels, praticables par tous les temps, nombreux étaient les entraîneurs qui amenaient leurs chevaux sur la plage lorsque les terrains d'herbe dont ils disposaient étaient gelés.

It's nice to win your own race. The 17th Earl of Derby greets his 1933 Derby victor Hyperion and jockey Tommy Weston. Lord Derby, who was the most prominent owner on the Turf, saw his famous black and white colours carried to an incredible twenty Classic victories.

Sieger im eigenen Rennen. Der 17. Earl von Derby beglückwünscht Hyperion und Jockey Tommy Weston zum 1933er Derby-Sieg. Der prominenteste aller Pferdebesitzer, Lord Derby, und seine berühmten schwarzweißen Stallfarben brachten es auf schier unglaubliche 20 Siege bei den klassischen Rennen.

C'est toujours agréable de gagner à domicile. Le 17ᵉ comte de Derby félicite son cheval Hyperion et le jockey Tommy Weston qui viennent d'emporter le Derby de 1933. Les célèbres couleurs de Lord Derby (noir et blanc), le propriétaire le plus en vue du monde du turf, ne totalisèrent pas moins de vingt victoires dans les classiques !

Say it with flowers. Draped in a garland, Broker's Tip, the winner of North America's most famous race, the Kentucky Derby, in 1933. Don Meade is the victorious rider. Blinkers, which are often worn by rogues in Europe, have always been used on genuine horses by American racehorse trainers.

Sag' es mit Blumen. Jockey Don Meade mit Broker's Tip, reich bekränzter Sieger des 1933er Kentucky Derbys, dem bekanntesten Rennen Nordamerikas. Scheuklappen, die in Europa bockigen Pferden angelegt wurden, waren in Amerika grundsätzlich im Gebrauch.

Dites-le avec des fleurs. Une couronne de fleurs pour Broker's Tip, monté par Don Meade et vainqueur en 1933 du Derby du Kentucky, la course la plus célèbre outre-Atlantique. En Europe, seuls les chevaux récalcitrants sont affublés d'œillères mais aux États-Unis, en revanche, les entraîneurs ont toujours eu coutume d'en équiper les chevaux de pure race.

The look of eagles. Phar Lap and jockey Jim Pike on the way to the start before winning the Melbourne Cup in Australia on 13 November 1930. New Zealand-born Phar Lap is still regarded as the best horse ever to have been bred in the Southern Hemisphere.

Adler-Blicke. Die späteren Sieger Phar Lap und Jockey Jim Pike vor dem Start im australischen Melbourne Cup am 13. November 1930. Der neuseeländische Phar Lap gilt noch heute als die beste Züchtung der Südhalbkugel.

Regards de prédateurs. Phar Lap et son jockey Jim Pike se dirigent vers le départ avant de gagner la Melbourne Cup, en Australie, 13 novembre 1930. Phar Lap, le cheval néo-zélandais, est aujourd'hui encore considéré comme le meilleur cheval jamais élevé dans l'hémisphère Sud.

Dramatic interlude. Actor-manager Tom Walls, family and friends admire April the Fifth, the horse he trained to win the 1932 Derby, at his home at Ewell in Surrey, 2 June 1932. As well as training a small string at Epsom, Walls was one of the best known light comedians on the London stage.

Kunstpause. Der Schauspieler und Theaterdirektor Tom Walls wirft im Kreise seiner Freunde und Familie einen anerkennenden Blick auf das Pferd April the Fifth, das er als Trainer 1932 zum Derby-Sieg führte. Neben seiner Tätigkeit als Trainer eines kleinen Stalls in Epsom war Walls einer der bekanntesten Komiker der Londoner Bühnen. Das Foto entstand am 2. Juni 1932 auf Walls Grundstück in Ewell, Surrey.

Intermède théâtral. Le manager et acteur Tom Walls chez lui, à Ewell, dans le Surrey, en compagnie de sa famille et de quelques amis admire April the Fifth, le cheval qu'il entraînait et qui devait remporter le Derby en 1932, 2 juin 1932. Parallèlement à ses activités d'entraîneur d'une petite écurie à Epsom, Walls était l'un des comédiens comiques les plus connus de la scène londonienne.

Where's that damn ukelele? Singer and comedian George Formby and his wife Beryl with Lucky Bert, the horse he was to ride in a hurdle race at Northholt Park, 13 November 1938. Like many stars of stage and screen, Formby was a great racing fan.

Wo war noch gleich die Ukulele? Der Sänger und Komiker George Formby, seine Frau Beryl und Lucky Bert, mit dem Formby an diesem 13. November 1938 das Hindernis-rennen in Northholt Park bestritt. Wie viele seiner Kollegen von Leinwand und Bühne war Formby ein großer Anhänger des Pferderennens.

Mais où est ce satané ukulélé ? Le chanteur et comédien George Formby et son épouse Beryl entourent Lucky Bert, que l'acteur allait monter pour une course de haies à Northholt Park, le 13 novembre 1938. À l'instar de nombreuses célébrités de la scène et du cinéma, Formby était un passionné des courses.

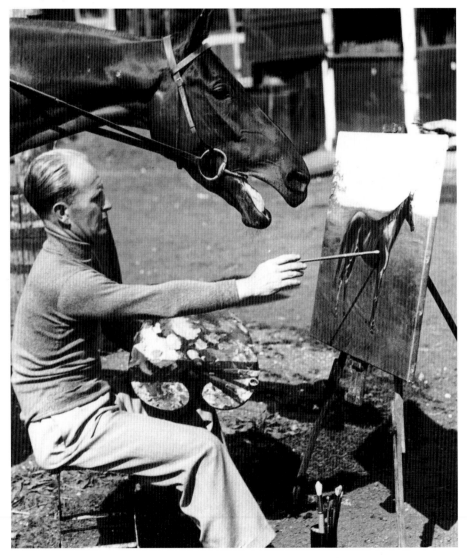

Pantomime horses.
(Opposite)
Racehorse Poverty
Street inspects his
likeness on the
artist's canvas,
21 August 1939.
(Right) Miss I
Croxton gets
some practice at
riding a finish,
10 October 1938.

Original und
Fälschung?!
(Gegenüber) Das
Rennpferd Poverty
Street überprüft, ob
sein Leinwandpor-
trät ihm ähnlich sieht,
21. August 1939.
(Rechts)
Miss I. Croxton übt
bereits für das Finish,
10. Oktober 1938.

Une réplique de
cheval. (Ci-contre)
Poverty Street,
le cheval de
course, examine
sa propre effigie sur
la toile de l'artiste,
21 août 1939.
(À droite)
Mlle I. Croxton
s'entraîne pour
l'arrivée de la course,
10 octobre 1938.

Travelling men. Top jockeys leave London from King's Cross Station for the start of the flat season. (Front row, left to right) Freddie Fox, Gordon Richards and Steve Donoghue. (Back row, left to right) Jock Burns, Fred Lane and Charlie Smirke, 25 March 1935.

Reisende soll man nicht aufhalten. Spitzenjockeys brechen vom Londoner Bahnhof King's Cross zum Start in die Galopp-Saison auf, 25. März 1935. Vordere Reihe von links nach rechts: Freddie Fox, Gordon Richards und Steve Donoghue. Hintere Reihe von links nach rechts: Jock Burns, Fred Lane und Charlie Smirke.

Des voyageurs. Les meilleurs jockeys britanniques réunis à King's Cross Station s'apprêtent à quitter Londres pour le début de la saison de plat, 25 mars 1935. (Au premier rang, de gauche à droite) Freddie Fox, Gordon Richards et Steve Donoghue. (Au second rang, de gauche à droite) Jock Burns, Fred Lane et Charlie Smirke.

Have horse will travel. Lo Zingare leaves the horsebox to enter a portable stall which will be hoisted aboard the Australia-bound SS *Port Alma*, 13 November 1934.

Klar Schiff zum Ab-legen. Lo Zingare wechselt von der Transportbox in einen Stallcontainer, um an Bord der SS *Port Alma* auf die Reise nach Aus-tralien zu gehen, 13. November 1934.

Qui veut aller loin ménage sa monture. Lo Zingare quitte son box pour entrer dans une stalle qui sera hissée à bord du SS *Port Alma,* prêt à appareiller pour l'Australie, le 13 novembre 1934.

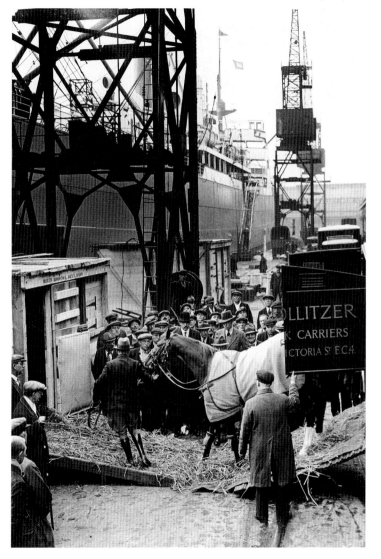

Train times. Runners for the Royal Meeting arrive by train at Ascot station, 15 June 1936. Before the invention of the motorised horsebox, horses always travelled by rail. Often, the stable lads walked their horses many miles from their training places to the nearest station.

Alles aussteigen. Die vierbeinigen Teilnehmer des Royal Meeting bei ihrer Ankunft am Bahnhof von Ascot am 15. Juni 1936. Bis zur Einführung motorisierter Pferdetransporte mussten die Tiere noch mit dem Zug reisen. Auf dem häufig kilometerweiten Weg vom Trainingsgelände bis zum nächsten Bahnhof wurden die Pferde von ihren Stalljungen begleitet.

L'ère du train. Les concurrents du Royal Meeting arrivent en train en gare d'Ascot, le 15 juin 1936. Avant l'invention des boxes tirés par des véhicules motorisés, les chevaux effectuaient toujours leurs déplacements en train. Il arrivait fréquemment que les garçons d'écurie parcourent de nombreux kilomètres pour amener leurs chevaux jusqu'à la gare la plus proche.

Busy bookmakers. Bookies erect their boards on the rails at Tattenham Corner on the morning before the 1934 Derby. In the good old days, punters had to beware that bookmakers in the cheaper Epsom enclosures did not welsh on winning bets and leave the racecourse without paying out.

Am Morgen vor dem Derby des Jahres 1934 stellen eifrige Buchmacher am Rand der Tattenham-Kurve ihre Schilder auf. In der „guten alten Zeit" mussten Wettende auf der Hut sein, dass die Buchmacher auf den billigeren Plätzen nicht mit ihrem Gewinn durchbrannten.

Des bookmakers affairés. Ces bookmakers installent leurs tableaux contre la balustrade le matin du Derby de 1934. Au bon vieux temps, les parieurs devaient veiller à ce que les bookmakers des secteurs les moins chers de l'hippodrome d'Epsom ne s'éclipsent sans honorer les paris gagnants.

A spread fit for a king. Workmen decorate the Royal Box at Ascot
with flowers in preparation for the Royal Meeting, 17 June 1935.
Up until 1939, Royal Ascot's four-day fixture was the only meeting
held at the Berkshire course.

Ein königliches Arrangement. Arbeiter dekorieren die königliche Loge
für das Royal Meeting, 17. Juni 1935. Bis 1939 wurde auf der
Berkshire-Strecke ausschließlich das viertägige Royal Meeting ausgetragen.

Une loge aux dimensions royales. Des employés fleurissent la loge
royale d'Ascot en prévision du Royal Meeting, 17 juin 1935. Jusqu'en
1939, la réunion de quatre jours du Royal Ascot était la seule
organisée à Berkshire.

All in a day's work. In front of empty stands groundsmen build the water jump at Aintree before the 1935 Grand National. Although the water jump is one of the smaller National fences, it is an obstacle which must be jumped perfectly. A careless foot in the water can ruin a fancied runner's chances.

Auf dem Sprung. Vor dem Hintergrund der leeren Tribünen bereiten Platzwarte den Wassergraben für die 1935er Grand National in Aintree vor. Obwohl dieser Sprung zu den leichteren Hindernissen des Rennens zählt, muss er perfekt gesprungen werden. Jeder Fehltritt kann die Chancen eines aussichtsreichen Teilnehmers zunichte machen.

La routine. Devant des tribunes vides, ces employés aménagent l'obstacle de la rivière à Aintree, avant le Grand National de 1935. Même si la haie représente l'un des plus bas obstacles du Grand National, il est important de ne pas commettre la moindre erreur : un sabot retombant malencontreusement dans l'eau peut ruiner tous les espoirs d'un concurrent.

Never believe what you read in the papers. (Above) Top jockeys Michael Beary (left) and Billy Nevett study the Royal Ascot card, June 1936. (Right) Tipster 'Prince' Raz Monolulu gives the police some inside information, June 1932.

Man muss nicht alles glauben, was in der Zeitung steht. (Oben) Die Spitzenjockeys Michael Beary (links) und Billy Nevett studieren das Royal-Ascot-Programm vom Juni 1936. (Rechts) Der Tippgeber „Prinz" Raz Monolulu versorgt die Polizei mit Insider-Informationen, Juni 1932.

Ne croyez jamais ce que disent les journaux. (Ci-dessus) Les jockeys Michael Beary (à gauche) et Billy Nevett étudient attentivement le programme du Royal Ascot du juin 1936. (À droite) Le pronostiqueur « Prince » Raz Monolulu livre de précieux renseignements à la police, juin 1932.

Jack the Lad. Brown Jack (H Lang up), who won Royal Ascot's Queen Alexandra Stakes six times, was the public's favourite horse between the wars. Brown Jack also won the Champion Hurdle before concentrating on flat racing, when he was usually partnered by Steve Donoghue.

Kumpel Jack. Brown Jack (hier mit Jockey H. Lang) gewann die Queen Alexandra Stakes von Royal Ascot sechs Mal und avancierte zwischen den Kriegen zum Publikumsliebling. Das Pferd siegte außerdem im Champion Hurdle, bevor es auf Flachrennen und zu Jockey Steve Donoghue überwechselte.

L'ami Jack. Brown Jack, monté par H. Lang, a remporté le Prix Queen Alexandra du Royal Ascot à six reprises. Il était le cheval favori du public durant l'entre-deux-guerres. Brown Jack a également remporté le Champion Hurdle (course de haies) avant de disputer exclusivement des courses de plat, au cours desquelles il était généralement monté par Steve Donoghue.

Keeping it in the family. Major Noël Furlong leads in his son Frank on Reynoldstown, the winner of 1935 Grand National. Reynoldstown took the 1936 National too, but ridden by Fulke Walwyn, later a leading jump trainer.

Der Apfel fällt nicht weit vom Stamm. Major Noël Furlong präsentiert seinen Sohn Frank auf Reynoldstown, frisch gebackener Sieger bei der Grand National von 1935. Reynoldstown gewann das Rennen auch 1936, diesmal mit Fulke Walwyn, dem späteren Erfolgstrainer für Hindernisrennen.

On reste en famille. Noël Furlong conduit son fils Frank, sur Reynoldstown, vainqueur du Grand National de 1935. Reynoldstown devait remporter également l'édition de 1936, monté cette fois par Fulke Walwyn qui allait devenir un entraîneur de premier plan pour les épreuves de saut.

Hunting folk. An admiring crowd watches jockey Cyril Buckham
unsaddle the Royal Hunt Cup winner, Colorado Kid, at Royal
Ascot, 14 June 1933. The Hunt Cup is the most competitive
handicap at the Royal Meeting and is always run on Wednesday,
the second day.

Jäger und Sammler. Das begeisterte Publikum umringt Colorado
Kid und Jockey Cyril Buckham beim Absatteln nach ihrem Sieg
im Royal Hunt Cup am 14. Juni 1933 beim Royal Ascot. Der
Hunt Cup ist das anspruchvollste Rennen beim Royal Meeting
und findet immer am Mittwoch, dem zweiten Tag, statt.

Le folklore de Hunt. Une foule admirative regarde le jockey
Cyril Buckham desseller Colorado Kid, le cheval vainqueur
de la Royal Hunt Cup au Royal Ascot, 14 juin 1933. La Hunt
Cup constitue le handicap le plus relevé du meeting royal et
se dispute toujours le mercredi, le deuxième jour.

Enchanting Epsom. An enormous crowd watches the Derby runners round Tattenham Corner in 1935. The race was won by Bahram, owned by the Aga Khan and ridden by Freddie Fox. Bahram was a colt of the highest class and also took the 1935 2,000 Guineas and St Leger.

Entzückendes Epsom. Eine gewaltige Zuschauermenge verfolgt die Teilnehmer des 1935er Derbys bei der Umrundung der Tattenham-Kurve. Sieger wurde Bahram, das Pferd des Aga Khan, mit Freddie Fox. Bahram, ein Rennpferd höchster Güte, holte sich 1935 auch die 2 000 Guineas und das St. Leger.

Le charme d'Epsom. Une foule immense regarde les concurrents du Derby de 1935 négocier le virage de Tattenham. C'est Bahram, le cheval de l'Aga Khan monté par Freddie Fox, qui a remporté la course. Bahram, poulain de grande classe, s'est également imposé cette même année lors du 2 000 Guinées et du Prix de St-Leger.

(Above) A circuit to go. The runners hug the rails in the Ascot Stakes at the Royal Meeting, 14 June 1937. (Opposite) In the shadow of the post. Gordon Richards and Pasch pull away from Fair Copy to land the Eclipse Stakes at Sandown Park, 15 July 1938.

(Oben) Noch eine Runde. Die Teilnehmer bei den Ascot Stakes im Rahmen des Royal Meetings gehen auf Tuchfühlung mit der Absperrung, 14. Juni 1937. (Gegenüber) Kurz vor dem Ziel. Gordon Richards und Pasch ziehen an Fair Copy vorbei und gewinnen am 15. Juli 1938 die Eclipse Stakes von Sandown Park.

(Ci-dessus) Encore un tour. Les participants se présent contre les balustrades lors du Prix d'Ascot dans le Royal Meeting du 14 juin 1937. (Ci-contre) Sur le poteau. Gordon Richards sur Pasch dépasse Fair Copy et remporte le Prix Eclipse au Sandown Park, le 15 juillet 1938.

Hello, hello. A policeman observes jockey J Ward's attempts to extricate his mount Donjeroo from an open ditch at the Cheltenham Festival, 9 March 1933. Cheltenham's three-day Festival Meeting, held in March, is the pinnacle of Britain's jump season, featuring the Gold Cup and the Champion Hurdle.

Aber hallo! Unter den Augen des Gesetzes versucht der Jockey J. Ward sein Pferd Donjeroo aus dem Graben von Cheltenham zu ziehen, 9. März 1933. Das dreitägige Cheltenham Festival Meeting im März bildet mit dem Gold Cup und dem Champion Hurdle den Saisonhöhepunkt der britischen Hindernisrennen.

Bonjour! Un policier observe les efforts du jockey J. Ward, qui tente d'extirper son cheval Donjeroo du fossé lors de la rencontre de Cheltenham, le 9 mars 1933. Le concours hippique qui comporte la Gold Cup et le Champion Hurdle est le plus important de ce genre. Il dure trois jours et se tient en mars.

Sitting on the fence.
W Parvin looks
bemused after
parting company
with Blue Prince in
the Grand National,
25 March 1938.
Parvin and Blue
Prince did much
better in 1935,
finishing second to
Reynoldstown.

Zaungäste. Etwas
verwirrt schaut
W. Parvin auf Blue
Prince, der ihn bei
der Grand National
vom 25. März 1938
abgeworfen hat.
1935 harmonierten
sie eindeutig besser
und wurden hinter
Reynoldstown
Zweite.

Assis sur la haie.
W. Parvin semble
perplexe après avoir
été désarçonné de
sa monture Blue
Prince dans le
Grand National,
le 25 mars 1938.
Parvin et Blue Prince
eurent plus de succès
en 1935, terminant
seconds derrière
Reynoldstown.

A woman's work is never done. A washerwoman checks that jockeys' silks and britches are in pristine condition before the valet takes the kit to the races. Valets often have to work late into the night to ensure their jockeys' equipment is spick and span for the next day's racing.

Die Arbeit einer Frau ist nie zu Ende. Eine Waschfrau überprüft den einwandfreien Zustand der Jockey-Kluften, bevor sie von Stallgehilfen zur Rennbahn gebracht werden. Damit die Ausrüstung der Jockeys am Renntag tadellos aussieht, müssen die Gehilfen oft bis spät in die Nacht arbeiten.

Le travail d'une femme n'est jamais terminé. Une lavandière vérifie que les casaques et les pantalons des jockeys sont d'une propreté irréprochable avant que les lads ne les transportent jusqu'au champ de courses. Ces derniers doivent souvent travailler jusque tard dans la nuit afin de garautir aux jockeys des tenues impeccables pour la course du lendemain.

A stitch in time. Seamstresses at Dr Gilbert's, the famous Newmarket colour-makers, sew new jockeys' silks and caps in preparation for the coming flat season, 7 March 1939. Major owners, like the Aga Khan and the 17th Earl of Derby, needed several sets of silks, as they often had runners at different meetings on the same day.

Nach Stich und Faden. Näherinnen in Dr. Gilberts berühmter Jockey-Schneiderei bereiten die Ausrüstung für die bevorstehende Galopp-Saison vor, 7. März 1939. Die großen Stalleigentümer wie der Aga Khan oder der 17. Earl von Derby brauchten oft mehrere Anzüge, weil ihre Pferde häufig am selben Tag bei verschiedenen Rennen an den Start gingen.

Un point de couture en vitesse. Les couturières de chez Dr Gilbert, la célèbre maison de Newmarket, mettent la dernière main aux casaques et aux toques des jockeys en vue de la prochaine saison de plat, 7 mars 1939. Les principaux propriétaires d'écurie, comme l'Aga Khan ou le 17e comte de Derby, qui alignaient plusieurs concurrents aux différents meetings d'une même journée, avaient besoin de plusieurs tenues.

How do I look, dear? Two elegant, extravagantly dressed ladies attract admiring glances from male racegoers on the second day of Royal Ascot, 14 June 1931. The exotic cocktail of *haute couture* and fast horses has always made the Royal Meeting the world's most photographed fixture.

Wie gefalle ich dir, Liebling? Zwei elegant und extravagant gekleidete Ladys ziehen bewundernde Blicke des männlichen Publikums auf sich. Das Bild entstand am 14. Juni 1931, dem zweiten Tag des Royal Ascot Meetings. Das Zusammenspiel von Haute Couture und schnellen Pferden macht das Royal Meeting seit jeher zum meistfotografierten Sportereignis der Welt.

J'ai l'air de quoi, ma chère ? Deux élégantes affichent des tenues extravagantes qui leur valent les regards admiratifs des turfistes en ce second jour du meeting d'Ascot, le 14 juin 1931. L'attrait conjugué de la haute couture et des chevaux de course explique que cet événement soit le rendez-vous favori des photographes.

Would you believe it? Spectators in the Tattersalls enclosure at Newmarket watch the action of the Chippenham Stakes in disbelieving silence as the previous year's St Leger winner, Scottish Union, is surprisingly beaten, May 1939. Scottish Union was trained in Wiltshire by Noël Cannon, who later brought the famous Australian jockey Scobie Breasley to ride in Britain.

Ist es zu glauben? Die Zuschauer auf der Tattersall-Tribüne verfallen in ungläubiges Schweigen, als Scottish Union – Vorjahressieger im St. Leger – bei den Chippenham Stakes überraschend geschlagen wird, Mai 1939. Scottish Union trainierte in Wiltshire bei Noël Cannon, der später den berühmten australischen Jockey Scobie Breasley auf die Insel holte.

Incroyable! Les spectateurs de l'enceinte de Tattersalls à Newmarket suivent le Prix de Chippenham dans un silence incrédule en réalisant que Scottish Union, vainqueur de St Leger l'année précédente, vient de se faire battre à la surprise générale, mai 1939. Scottish Union était entraîné dans le Wiltshire par Noël Cannon, qui allait plus tard ramener le fameux jockey australien Scobie Breasley en Grande-Bretagne.

Summer in the country. Ascot racegoers walk from the station through fields and beneath trees to reach the Royal Enclosure on a sweltering afternoon, 17 June 1939.

Eine Landpartie im Sommer. Ascot-Zuschauer marschieren querfeldein vom Bahnhof zur Rennbahn in der nachmittäglichen Hitze, 17. Juni 1939.

L'été à la campagne. Les turfistes d'Ascot arrivent de la gare et, à travers les champs et les bois, se dirigent par une chaleur accablante vers l'hippodrome royal, 17 juin 1939.

Spring in their stride. A leafy umbrella shades spectators as they watch the field for the Brentford Selling Stakes run into the straight at Kempton Park, 16 April 1938. Kempton, a leading British dual-purpose track, now hosts one of the jump season's most prestigious races, the King George VI Chase, run on Boxing Day.

Frühlingshafter Schwung. Unter einem Schatten spendenden Blätterdach verfolgen die Zuschauer das Feld der Brentford Selling Stakes von Kempton Park beim Einbiegen auf die Schlussgerade, 16. April 1938. Kempton gilt als eine der führenden britischen Mehrzweck-Bahnen. Inzwischen wird auf der Strecke an jedem zweiten Weihnachtsfeiertag das King George VI. Chase ausgetragen, eines der wichtigsten Jagdrennen der Saison.

Une foulée printanière. Protégé lés du soleil par les arbres les spectateurs du Prix Brentford Selling regardent les concurrents aborder la ligne droite de Kempton Park, l'un des principaux hippodromes britanniques pour les courses d'obstacles et de plat, 16 avril 1938. Aujourd'hui, l'une des plus prestigieuses courses d'obstacles, le steeple-chase King George VI, s'y dispute le lendemain de Noël.

Mobile stewards. Stewards keep a weather eye on the runners
throughout a race, 26 September 1938. These were the days before
patrol cameras, which were to make officials' jobs much easier.

Mobile Ordnungskräfte. Rennbeobachter werfen einen genauen Blick
auf das Geschehen, 26. September 1938. Die spätere Einführung von
Überwachungskameras bedeutete eine immense Arbeitserleichterung
für die Funktionäre.

Des organisateurs mobiles. Les organisateurs surveillent les concurrents
tout au long de la course, 26 septembre 1938. Les caméras mobiles
n'existaient pas encore. Par la suite, elles allaient faciliter grandement
le travail des officiels.

Afternoon all. A police car escorts a string of racehorses trained by Fred
Templeman at Lambourn in Berkshire during a strike by four hundred stable
staff, 23 May 1938. The staff were replaced by volontary helpers.

Nachmittagsspaziergang. Die Polizei eskortiert eine Gruppe von Rennpferden
während eines Streikes, 23. Mai 1938. Die 400 streikenden Angestellten von
Trainer Fred Templeman in Lambourn, Berkshire, wurden durch freiwillige
Helfer ersetzt.

L'après-midi du 23 mai 1938. En raison d'une grève de quatre cents
employés des écuries, une voiture de police escorte cette colonne de chevaux
de course entraînés par Fred Templeman à Lambourn, dans le Berkshire. Le
personnel fut remplacé par des bénévoles.

(Above) Dividend calculators check win and place bets on the Tote in 1939. (Opposite, above left) A lady uses the money-in-the-slot Tote at Aintree (Opposite, above right) Roving staff pay out the winnings. (Opposite, below) Betting on the two shilling Tote.

(Oben) Im Totalisator-Büro wird die Dividende für Platz und Sieg errechnet, 1939. (Gegenüber, oben links) Eine Lady in Aintree bedient den Münz-Totalisator. (Gegenüber, oben rechts) Ein Rennbahn-Angestellter zahlt die Gewinne aus. (Gegenüber, unten) Am Ausgabeschalter der Zwei-Schilling-Wetten.

(Ci-dessus) Calcul, chez un bookmaker, des gains revenant aux parieurs, 1939. (Ci-contre, en haut à gauche) Une dame utilise les machines automatiques d'Aintree. (Ci-contre, en haut à droite) Paiement des gains par le personnel mobile. (Ci-contre, en bas) Des paris au guichet à deux shillings de chez Tote.

4. Riding the storm
Im Sturm
Dans la tempête

A legend in his lifetime. Gordon Richards takes the 2,000 Guineas winner Tudor Minstrel to post for the 1947 Eclipse Stakes. In a long and distinguished career, Richards was the British champion flat jockey a record-breaking twenty-six times and rode many winners in the royal colours.

Eine Legende schon zu Lebzeiten. Gordon Richards führt den 2 000 Gunieas-Sieger Tudor Minstrel an den Start der Eclipse Stakes von 1947. In seiner langen und einzigartigen Karriere brachte es Richards auf die Rekordzahl von 26 britischen Jockey-Championaten und ritt zahlreiche Siegerpferde in den königlichen Farben.

Une légende de son vivant. Gordon Richards emmène Tudor Minstrel, vainqueur des 2 000 Guinées, à la victoire dans le Prix Eclipse de 1947. Richards fit une carrière éblouissante, s'imposant à 26 reprises comme le meilleur jockey britannique sur le plat, ce qui constitue un record et montant de nombreux chevaux gagnants pour le compte de la famille royale.

In England in the early Forties, American forces laid concrete over Newbury's hallowed turf and racecourse stables housed prisoners instead of horses. Britain was at war again and racing struggled on at a vastly reduced scale. The Derby was run at Newmarket rather than Epsom but racegoers, anxious for relief from the bombs and the sirens, attended wartime fixtures in droves. They cheered with patriotic zeal when King George VI won four Classics with Big Game and Sun Chariot in 1942. With the advent of war, international racing ceased but, when the cross-Channel transportation of horses resumed in 1945, it was clear that Marcel Boussac's French studs had not only survived but had thrived during the German Occupation. In the immediate post-war years, Boussac's horses launched a devastating assault on big English races. In Germany, however, racing had failed to prosper. Much of the German bloodstock was dispersed, or fell into Russian hands, and the National Stud at Graditz and the great racecourse at Hoppegarten were lost behind the Iron Curtain. A young Irish trainer, Vincent O'Brien, set the jumping world alight with a string of important victories over fences and hurdles. He would later devote his talents to flat racing and become a racing legend.

In den frühen vierziger Jahren planierten amerikanische Truppen den heiligen, englischen Rasen der Rennbahn von Newbury und die Ställe wurden zu Zellen für Kriegsgefangene umfunktioniert. Schließlich führte Großbritannien Krieg, und so musste der Pferderennsport seine Aktivitäten deutlich einschränken. Das Derby fand nicht wie üblich in Epsom sondern in Newmarket statt. Dennoch kamen die Besucher in Scharen zu den Wettbewerben der Kriegszeit; das Pferderennen bot eine ersehnte Abwechslung von Bomben und Sirenen. Mit patriotischem Eifer jubelte das Publikum König George VI. zu, als er 1942 mit seinen Pferden Big Game und Sun Chariot vier klassische Rennen gewann. Der internationale Pferderennsport wurde mit Beginn des Krieges zwar eingestellt. Als 1945 der Tiertransport über den Ärmelkanal wieder in Gang kam, wurde allerdings schnell klar, dass die französischen Zuchtpferde Marcel Boussacs die deutsche Besatzung überlebt hatten. Mehr noch, sie hatten sich prächtig entwickelt. In den unmittelbaren Nachkriegsjahren bliesen Boussacs Pferde zu einem verheerenden Angriff auf die großen englischen Rennen. In Deutschland dagegen erlitt der Pferderennsport empfindliche Rückschläge: Die meisten der deutschen Vollblüter wurden über das Land verstreut oder fielen in russische Hand. Das preußische Hauptgestüt von Graditz und die berühmte Rennbahn Hoppegarten verschwanden hinter dem eisernen Vorhang. Währenddessen bereicherte der junge irische Trainer Vincent O'Brien die Welt des Springreitens mit einer ganzen Reihe wichtiger Siege. Später widmete er seine Talente dem Flachrennen und sollte zu einer Legende des Pferderennsports werden.

En Angleterre, en ce début des années quarante, les forces armées américaines bétonnaient les écuries du sacro-saint champ de course de Newbury les transformant en cellules pour des prisonniers de guerre. Cette nouvelle guerre dans laquelle étaient engagés les Britanniques s'accompagna d'une baisse sensible du nombre des courses hippiques. Le Derby se courait alors à Newmarket plutôt qu'à Epsom mais les turfistes, soucieux de se sauver du bruit des sirènes se rendaient en masse aux courses. C'est avec un zèle tout patriotique qu'ils applaudirent Big Game et Sun Chariot, les chevaux du roi George VI, gagnants de quatre classiques en 1942. Le déclenchement de la guerre mit fin aux courses internationales mais lorsque, en 1945, les chevaux d'Europe continentale revinrent en Grande-Bretagne, il apparut clairement que les haras français de Marcel Boussac n'avaient pas seulement survécu durant l'occupation allemande mais qu'ils avaient même prospéré. Pendant les premières années ayant suivi la guerre, les chevaux de Boussac raflèrent les plus grands prix britanniques. Par contre, le monde des courses en Allemagne était loin d'afficher la même santé. La plupart des chevaux de race allemands étaient dispersés sur le territoire ou étaient tombés entre les mains des Russes. De plus, les haras nationaux de Graditz et le célèbre champ de course de Hoppegarten se trouvaient dès lors de l'autre côté du rideau de fer. Vincent O'Brien, un jeune entraîneur irlandais, collectionnait les victoires dans les courses d'obstacles. Plus tard, il devait se consacrer aux courses de plat et deviendrait une légende dans le monde des courses.

(Above) A genius at work. Gordon Richards puts King George VI's 1942 2,000 Guineas winner Big Game through his paces. (Right) All the King's men. Stable lads exercise King George VI's horses on the Wiltshire Downs at Fred Darling's stables at Beckhampton, 6 June 1942.

(Oben) Ein Genie bei der Arbeit. Gordon Richards beim Training auf Big Game. Das Pferd des Königs George VI. holte 1942 die 2 000 Guineas. (Rechts) Königlicher Ausritt. Stalljungen trainieren die Pferde George VI. auf den Hügeln von Wiltshire bei Fred Darlings Stallungen in Beckhampton, 6. Juni 1942.

(Ci-dessus) Un génie en action. Gordon Richards effectue un galop d'essai avec Big Game, le vainqueur du 2 000 Guinées de 1942 appartenant au roi George VI. (À droite) Les lads du roi à l'entraînement avec les chevaux dans les collines du Wiltshire, aux alentours des écuries de Fred Darling à Beckhampton, le 6 juin 1942.

A king and his queen. King George VI in Royal Air Force uniform leads in Sun Chariot and Gordon Richards after winning the Oaks at Newmarket, 13 June 1942. Sun Chariot also took the 1,000 Guineas and St Leger.

Der König und seine Königin. König George VI. in Royal-Air-Force-Uniform führt Sun Chariot und Gordon Richards nach ihrem Sieg bei den Oaks in Newmarket von der Bahn, 13. Juni 1942. Sun Chariot holte sich außerdem die 1 000 Guineas und das St. Leger.

Un roi et sa reine. Le roi George VI, en uniforme de la Royal Air Force, conduit Sun Chariot et Gordon Richards après leur victoire dans les Oaks de Newmarket, 13 juin 1942. Sun Chariot devait également remporter le 1 000 Guinées et le Prix de St Leger.

The master and his pupil. Trainer Fred Darling with the 1942 2,000 Guineas winner Big Game, 6 June 1942. Darling was reputed to administer small doses of arsenic to make his horses' coats shine brilliantly.

Der Lehrmeister und sein Schüler. Trainer Fred Darling mit Big Game, Sieger der 1942er 2 000 Guineas, 6. Juni 1942. Darling benutzte angeblich kleinere Mengen Arsen, um das Fell seiner Pferde zum Glänzen zu bringen.

Le maître et l'élève. L'entraîneur Fred Darling et Big Game, vainqueur du 2 000 Guinées en 1942, 6 juin 1942. Darling était connu pour administrer à ses chevaux de petites doses d'arsenic qui leur permettaient d'avoir une robe brillante.

Fighting it out. Bogskar (on the right) is just ahead of the runner-up, MacMoffat, at the last fence in the National, 5 April 1940. Bogskar was owned and trained by Lord Stalbridge at Eastbury in Berkshire.

Kopf-an-Kopf-Duell beim letzten Hindernis der Grand National am 5. April 1940. Bogskar (rechts) konnte seinen minimalen Vorsprung vor Verfolger MacMoffat ins Ziel retten. Bogskar gehörte Lord Stalbridge, der das Pferd in Eastbury, Berkshire, auch trainierte.

Bogskar (à droite) est en pleine bagarre et précèdant de peu MacMoffat, saute la dernière haie du Grand National, 5 avril 1940. Lord Stalbridge, installé à Eastbury, dans le Berkshire, était à la fois le propriétaire et entraîneur de Bogskar.

On leave. ATS girls cheer on the wartime National winner Bogskar, ridden by a forces' colleague, Flight Lieutenant Mervyn Jones, 5 April 1940. Sadly Jones never returned from an aerial bombing raid two years later.

Aufbruch. Mitglieder der „Organisation der weiblichen Angehörigen der Streitkräfte" (ATS) bejubeln den National-Sieger Bogskar, 5. April 1940. Das Pferd wurde von ihrem Kameraden, Leutnant Mervyn Jones geritten, der zwei Jahre darauf von einem Luftangriff nicht zurückkehrte.

En perm'. Des membres de l'ATS encouragent Bogskar, vainqueur du Grand National en ces temps de guerre, monté par un collègue des forces armées, le capitaine de l'armée de l'air Mervyn Jones, 5 avril 1940. Hélas, deux ans plus tard, Jones ne rentrera pas d'un raid aérien.

(Previous spread) Cavalry charge. A wartime Derby at Newmarket in 1941. The eventual winner, Owen Tudor, is hidden behind a wall of horses. War and peace. (Above) Spectators enjoying the sun on the Devil's Dyke at Newmarket during Owen Tudor's Derby win, 18 June 1941. (Left) Airmen line the course at Newmarket as Sam Wragg and Pont l'Évêque pass the post as winners of the 1940 Derby.

(Vorherige Doppelseite) Kavallerie-Sturm. Das Derby in Newmarket im Kriegsjahr 1941. Der spätere Sieger Owen Tudor ist hinter den anderen Pferden versteckt. Krieg und Frieden. (Oben) Die Zuschauer am Devil's Dyke genießen das gute Wetter in Newmarket bei Owen Tudors Derby-Sieg am 18. Juni 1941. (Links) Soldaten der Luftwaffe säumen die Rennbahn beim Derby des Jahres 1940 in Newmarket. Sam Wragg und Pont l'Évêque beendeten das Rennen als Sieger.

(Pages précédentes) La charge de la cavalerie. 1941. Derby en temps de guerre à Newmarket. Le vainqueur, Owen Tudor, est caché par le groupe de chevaux. Guerre et paix. (Ci-dessus) Les spectateurs, juchés sur la « Digue du Diable », profitent du soleil lors du Derby remporté par Owen Tudor à Newmarket, le 18 juin 1941. (À gauche) Les aviateurs sont alignés le long de la piste à Newmarket, tandis que Sam Wragg sur Pont l'Évêque, passe le poteau d'arrivée en vainqueur lors du Derby de 1940.

French connection.
(Left) Elegant
Parisian ladies
attend the first
French race meeting
to be held after the
Liberation,
October 1944.
(Opposite) Pearl
Diver and George
Bridgland win the
Derby for France,
7 June 1947.

French Connection.
(Links) Elegante
Pariser Damen beim
ersten französischen
Rennen nach der
Befreiung im
Oktober 1944.
(Gegenüber) George
Bridgland und Pearl
Diver holen am
7. Juni 1947 das
Derby für Frankreich.

La « french connec-
tion ». (À gauche)
D'élégantes Parisien-
nes vont assister à la
première course
disputée après la
Libération, en
octobre 1944.
(Ci-contre) Pearl
Diver et George
Bridgland rempor-
tent le Derby pour la
France le 7 juin 1947.

No ... 85 ...
or Boxe ... llowed
in this Enclosure

Go on, girls. Two-year-old fillies at the starting gate at Belmont Park racecourse, New York, 13 May 1946. Unlike their European counterparts, the Americans run most of their races on dirt rather than turf.

Auf geht's, Mädels. Zweijährige Stutenfohlen an der Startmaschine auf der New Yorker Rennbahn Belmont Park, 13. Mai 1946. Anders als in Europa werden die meisten amerikanischen Rennen auf Erde statt auf Rasen ausgetragen.

Allez les filles! Des juments de deux ans au départ d'une course à l'hippodrome de Belmont Park, à New York, 13 mai 1946. À la différence des courses européennes, la plupart des courses aux États-Unis se déroulent sur de la terre et non pas sur de la pelouse.

King James. Jockey Basil James on Alsab after winning the Preakness Stakes at Pimlico racecourse, Baltimore, Maryland, 9 May 1942. The Preakness is the second leg of the American Triple Crown between the Kentucky Derby and the Belmont Stakes.

König James. Der Jockey Basil James auf Alsab nach ihrem Sieg bei den Preakness Stakes, auf der Rennbahn vom Pimlico in Baltimore, Maryland, 9. Mai 1942. Neben dem Kentucky Derby und den Belmont Stakes sind die Preakness Stakes die dritte Konkurrenz der amerikanischen Triple Crown.

Le roi James. Le jockey Basil James, sur Alsab, vient de remporter le Prix de Preakness à l'hippodrome de Pimlico à Baltimore, dans le Maryland, 9 mai 1942. Ce prix constitue la seconde manche de la Triple Crown américaine et se déroule entre le Derby du Kentucky et le Prix de Belmont.

Skating on thin ice. The start of a race on the Obersee
at Arosa in Switzerland, 23 March 1946. Racing also
takes place on the frozen lake at St Moritz. Horses wear
special shoes with protruding studs to prevent them
slipping on the ice, which is harrowed to provide a
rougher surface with more grip.

Auf dünnem Eis. Rennstart auf dem Obersee im schwei-
zerischen Arosa, 23. März 1946. Auf dem gefrorenen
See von St. Moritz werden ebenfalls Rennen ausgetragen. Um ein Ausrutschen zu verhindern, tragen die
Pferde spezielle Hufen mit Stollen. Zusätzlich wird
das Eis aufgeraut, damit die Tiere einen besseren Halt
haben.

Du patinage sur une fine couche de glace. Départ d'une
course sur l'Obersee à Arosa, en Suisse. Des courses
sont également organisées sur le lac glacé de St Moritz,
23 mars 1946. Les chevaux sont équipés de fers
spéciaux, rehaussés de crampons saillants les empêchant
de glisser sur la glace hersée pour offrir donc une
meilleure adhérence.

Heat wave. With Glorious Goodwood living up to its reputation, a party of racegoers protect their heads from the blistering sun with pocket handkerchiefs, 30 July 1947. Sumptuous picnics and copious amounts of beer were the traditional fare for visitors to the Trundle Hill enclosure.

Hitzewelle. Glorious Goodwood wird seinem „heißen" Ruf einmal mehr gerecht. Mit Taschentüchern schützen sich diese Rennbesucher vor der sengenden Sonne, 30. Juli 1947. Ein reichhaltiges Picknick und große Mengen Bier gehörten traditionell zur Ausrüstung der Zuschauer auf den Rängen von Trundle Hill.

Une vague de chaleur. Glorious Goodwood est à la hauteur de sa réputation et certains spectateurs se protègent du soleil torride avec de simples mouchoirs, 30 juillet 1947. Les spectateurs du Trundle Hill avaient coutume d'organiser de somptueux pique-niques arrosés de larges quantités de bière.

Boiling bookie
offers hot odds.
The following day
Bill Williams has
to remove his
shirt to cope with
the sweltering
temperatures at
Goodwood.

Kochender Buch-
macher bietet
heiße Wetten.
Der schwitzende
Buchmacher Bill
Williams hat sich
am folgenden Tag
in der Hitze von
Goodwood seines
Hemdes entledigt.

Bookmaker en ébul-
lition offre des cotes
intéressantes. Le jour
suivant à Goodwood,
Bill Williams se voit
obligé de retirer sa
chemise pour sup-
porter la chaleur
accablante.

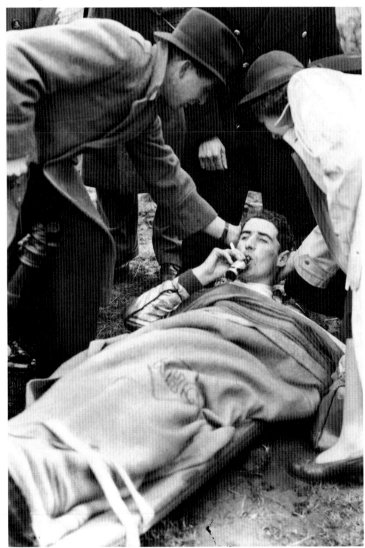

Irish whiskey. Irish jockey Aubrey Brabazon takes a medicinal swig of the hard stuff, and a calming cigarette, after falling from his National mount at Becher's Brook, 29 March 1947.

Irischer Whiskey. Der irische Jockey Aubrey Brabazon gönnt sich einen therapeutischen Schluck Hochprozentiges und eine beruhigende Zigarette nachdem er am Hindernis Becher's Brook bei der Grand National abgeworfen wurde, 29. März 1947.

Du whisky irlandais. Le jockey irlandais Aubrey Brabazon a bien besoin d'une gorgée de potion magique et d'une cigarette pour se remettre d'une chute lors du Grand National à Becher's Brook, 29 mars 1947.

There's no such thing as a poor bookmaker. Bill Beasley counts his winnings on the kitchen table after another successful day, 5 July 1949. Street bookies like Beasley employed runners to take bets for workers in Britain's towns and cities before the legalisation of betting shops in the Sixties.

Arme Buchmacher existieren nicht. Nach einem erfolgreichen Tag zählt der Buchmacher Bill Beasley seine Gewinne am Küchentisch, 5. Juli 1949. Vor Einführung der Wettbüros in den Sechzigern beschäftigten Buchmacher wie Beasley Laufburschen, die durch die Dörfer und Städte Großbritanniens zogen, um der arbeitenden Bevölkerung Wetten anzubieten.

Les bookmakers pauvres n'existent pas. Bill Beasley fait le compte de ses gains sur la table de la cuisine après un nouveau jour faste, 5 juillet 1949. Les bookmakers comme Beasley employaient des coursiers qui collectaient les paris des ouvriers dans les villes britanniques, avant la légalisation des officines de paris dans les années soixante.

The camera never lies. Nimbus (centre), ridden by Charlie Elliott, narrowly wins the Derby by a head from Amour Drake (right) and Swallow Tail, 4 June 1949. This was the first time that a photo-finish camera was used to place the first three home in the Derby.

Die Kamera lügt nicht. Nimbus (Mitte, mit Jockey Charlie Elliott) gewinnt denkbar knapp das Derby mit einem Kopf Vorsprung vor Amour Drake (rechts) und Swallow Tail. Dieses Derby vom 4. Juni 1949 war das erste, bei dem eine Fotofinish-Kamera zur Ermittlung der ersten drei Plätze zum Einsatz kam.

L'image ne trompe pas. Nimbus (au centre), monté par Charlie Elliott, remporte d'une tête le Derby devant Amour Drake (à droite) et Swallow Tail, 4 juin 1949. Pour la première fois lors de ce Derby, l'ordre d'arrivée des trois premiers était déterminé par une photographie.

Picture Post, finishing post. Two speeding American horses caught by the photo-finish camera, a mechanical eye that made it possible to split close finishers, 28 August 1948.

Die Titelseite der *Picture Post* vom 28. August 1948. Zwei amerikanische Sprintpferde im Focus der Zielkamera, die es ermöglicht, bei zeitgleichem Zieleinlauf den Sieger zu bestimmen.

La photographie d'arrivée du *Picture Post* du 28 août 1948. Deux chevaux photographiés à pleine vitesse sur la ligne d'arrivée. Cette nouvelle technique permit de déterminer le gagnant.

(Left) American champion jockey Johnny Longden and his wife on board the *Queen Elizabeth* at Southampton Docks, 25 August 1947. (Opposite) Twelve-year-old Lester Piggott at his father Keith's Lambourn stable in Berkshire, August 1948.

(Links) Der amerikanische Jockey Champion Johnny Longden mit seiner Frau an Bord der *Queen Elizabeth* am 25. August 1947 in Southampton. (Gegenüber) Der zwölfjährige Lester Piggott bei den Stallungen seines Vaters Keith in Lambourn, Berkshire, August 1948.

(À gauche) Le jockey américain Johnny Longden avec son épouse sont à bord du *Queen Elizabeth*, à Southampton, 25 août 1947. (Ci-contre) Lester Piggott, à l'âge de 12 ans dans l'écurie de son père Keith Lambourn, dans le Berkshire, août 1948.

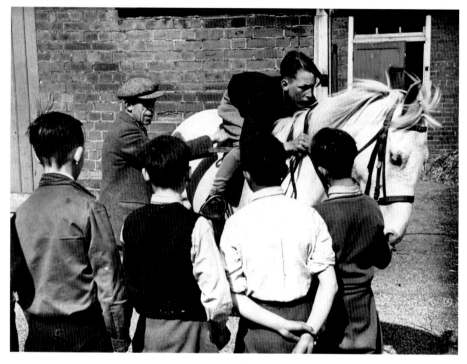

Learning the trade. (Above) Newmarket trainer Harry Wragg teaches his apprentices to ride a finish on the stable pony, May 1949. (Opposite) A tiny stable lad oils the hooves of the Derby winner Dante at his Middleham stable in North Yorkshire, 9 June 1945.

Lehrjahre. (Oben) Harry Wragg, Trainer in Newmarket, übt mit seinen Schülern den Schluss-Sprint auf einem Stallpony, Mai 1949. (Gegenüber) Ein kleiner Stalljunge ölt die Hufen des Derby-Siegers Dante in seinem Stall in Middleham, North Yorkshire, 9. Juni 1945.

L'apprentissage du métier. (Ci-dessus) Harry Wragg, l'entraîneur de Newmarket, enseigne à ses apprentis montés sur le poney du manège comment s'y prendre lors d'une arrivée, mai 1949. (Ci-contre) Un tout jeune garçon d'écurie huile les sabots de Dante, le vainqueur du Derby, dans son écurie de Middleham, ville située dans le Nord du Yorkshire, 9 juin 1945.

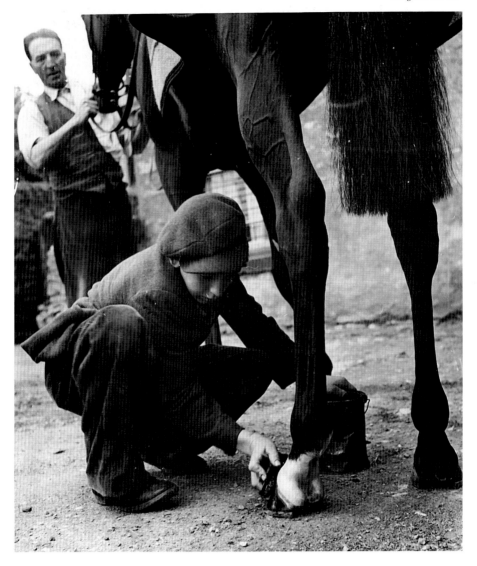

A weighty problem. Jump jockey Raymond Cane anxiously checks the scales, 20 March 1948.
A jockey must return after a race and weigh-in with the same weight with which he set out.
Any discrepancy at the weigh-in can cause a horse to be disqualified on technical grounds.

Ein gewichtiges Problem. Der Hindernis-Jockey Raymond Cane bei der Gewichtskontrolle
am 20. März 1948. Jeder Jockey wird vor und nach dem Rennen gewogen. Treten dabei
Gewichtsunterschiede zu Tage, kann sein Pferd wegen technischen Vergehens disqualifiziert
werden.

Un problème de poids. Le jockey Raymond Cane consulte la balance avec anxiété,
20 mars 1948. Après chaque course, le jockey doit remonter sur la balance et peser
exactement le même poids qu'avant la course. Toute différence de poids constatée à ce
moment-là peut entraîner la disqualification du cheval.

Jockeys' valet Joe
Ballinger fills a weight
cloth with the right
amount of lead,
22 March 1948.
It is the valet's
responsibility to
ensure that his rider
carries the correct
weight in every race.

Der Jockey-Gehilfe
Joe Ballinger bestückt
eine Bleiweste,
22. März 1948. Die
Gehilfen müssen
sicher stellen, dass
die Reiter in jedem
Rennen das korrek-
te Gewicht auf die
Waage bringen.

Joe Ballinger, assis-
tant du jockey,
leste un vêtement
de la quantité appro-
priée de plomb,
22 mars 1948. C'est
lui qui a la respons-
abilité de s'assurer
que le jockey pèse le
poids requis.

The Minstrel's Gallery. Gordon Richards wins the
2,000 Guineas at Newmarket on Mr J A Dewar's Tudor
Minstrel by a staggering eight lengths, 30 April 1947.
Tudor Minstrel started a hot favourite for the Derby
but failed to settle and could only finish fourth. Never-
theless, he was one of the best milers ever to set foot
on a racecourse.

Galavorstellung. Mit erstaunlichen acht Längen Vor-
sprung gewinnt Gordon Richards auf Tudor Minstrel
am 30. April 1947 die 2 000 Guineas in Newmarket.
Das Pferd aus dem Besitz von Mr. J. A. Dewar ging auch
als Favorit ins Derby, fand dort aber nicht zu seinem
Rhythmus und wurde nur Vierter. Trotzdem war Tudor
Minstrel über die Meilen-Distanz eines der besten
Pferde aller Zeiten.

Un triomphe. Gordon Richards remporte le 2 000
Guinées à Newmarket sur Tudor Minstrel, le cheval de
M J. A. Dewar qui a une avance phénoménale de huit
longueurs sur ses rivaux, 30 avril 1947. Tudor Minstrel
était grand favori au départ du Derby mais ne parvint
pas à se placer correctement et n'obtint que la
quatrième place. Il n'en était pas moins l'un des plus
rapides chevaux de tous les temps sur le mile.

(Above) I've seen it all before. A stern-faced Marcel Boussac and French Derby winner Sandjar, 1947. (Left) Back in business. A parade before the start at Hoppegarten racecourse near Berlin, where racing had just started again after the Second World War, 25 April 1949. (Following spread) Lady luck. Sheila's Cottage in the foreground carrying number 22, the eventual winner of the Grand National, 20 March 1948.

(Oben) Alles schon einmal da gewesen. Der finster dreinblickende Marcel Boussac mit Sandjar, dem Siegerpferd des französischen Derbys von 1947. (Links) Wieder im Geschäft. Die Parade vor dem Start auf der Rennbahn von Hoppegarten bei Berlin nach der Zwangspause durch den Zweiten Weltkrieg, 25. April 1949. (Folgende Doppelseite) Eine Dame im Glück. Sheila's Cottage (im Vordergrund, mit der Nummer 22) bei ihrem Grand-National-Sieg am 20. März 1948 in einer frühen Phase des Rennens.

(Ci-dessus) Déjà vu. Le visage sévère de Marcel Boussac, conduisant ici Sandjar, le vainqueur français du Derby en 1947. (À gauche) L'activité reprend. Un défilé avant le début du meeting sur l'hippodrome d'Hoppegarten près de Berlin, après la Seconde Guerre mondiale, 25 avril 1949. (Pages suivantes) Le numéro de la chance. Au premier plan, Sheila's Cottage porte le numéro vingt-deux qui s'imposera lors du Grand National du 20 mars 1948.

5. The old and the new
Zwischen Gestern und Morgen
En route vers la modernité

Roll on Royal Ascot. Fifteen-year-old apprentice jockey Lester Piggott about to ride out at his father Keith's stable two days after Christmas, 27 December 1950. Before the advent of all-weather racetracks in 1989 there was no flat racing in Britain during the winter, but flat race horses still needed to be exercised.

Royal Ascot kann kommen. Der 15-jährige Nachwuchs-Jockey Lester Piggott vor einem Ausritt auf dem Stall-Gelände seines Vaters Keith am 27. Dezember 1950. Vor 1989, als die ersten Allwetter-Rennbahnen aufkamen, fanden in Großbritannien im Winter keine Flachrennen statt. Dennoch mussten die Pferde trainiert werden.

Objectif : le Royal Ascot. Lester Piggott, un apprenti-jockey de 15 ans, se prépare à monter un cheval de l'écurie de son père Keith, deux jours après Noël, 27 décembre 1950. Avant la création en 1989 d'hippodromes utilisables en toute saison, aucune course de plat n'était organisée en Grande-Bretagne pendant l'hiver ; toutefois les chevaux devaient s'entraîner aussi en cette saison.

In 1953 Gordon Richards was knighted for services to racing and, days later, captured that elusive first Derby on Pinza. In 1954 the new golden boy of race-riding, eighteen-year-old Lester Piggott, followed in the footsteps of Sir Gordon Richards, winning on the outsider Never Say Die. Royalty's affection for and association with racing remained undiminished. Her Majesty Queen Elizabeth II won the 2,000 Guineas in 1958 with Pall Mall, but the Queen Mother was not so lucky. Her steeplechaser, Devon Loch, mysteriously collapsed on the run-in when well clear of the field in the 1956 Grand National. In the 1950s, jumping also had its high points. Sir Ken, widely believed to be the finest hurdler of all time, took three Champion Hurdles in a row. Sadly, the decade will also be remembered for skulduggery. Alcide, the heavily backed 1958 Derby favourite, was cruelly injured in his stable and forced to miss the race. Although the assailants were never found, unscrupulous bookmakers were widely believed to be responsible. On the Continent, Federico Tesio worked the oracle again. Although he never lived to see Ribot race, the Italian genius has gone down in history as the breeder of one of the best thoroughbreds ever. Ribot, who won two Arc de Triomphes with consummate ease, was an undisputed and unbeaten champion.

Im Jahre 1953 wurde Gordon Richards aufgrund seiner Verdienste für das Pferderennen zum Ritter geschlagen. Nur Tage später gelang ihm auf Pinza der so lang ersehnte Derby-Sieg. In die Fußstapfen Sir Gordon Richards' trat ein Jahr später der 18-jährige Lester Piggott. Der neue Goldjunge des Pferderennsports siegte 1954 auf dem Außenseiter Never Say Die. Die Liebe und die Verbindung der Royal Family zum Pferdesport war indes ungebrochen: Ihre Majestät Königin Elizabeth II. gewann 1958 die 2 000 Guineas mit Pall Mall. Die Königinmutter hatte jedoch weniger Glück. Ihr Hindernisrennpferd Devon Loch stürzte völlig unerklärlich auf der Zielgeraden bei der Grand National von 1956 – das Feld weit hinter sich. Auch die Hindernisrennen der Fünfziger waren reich an Höhepunkten. So gewann Sir Ken, den viele für den besten Hindernisreiter aller Zeiten halten, drei Championate in Folge. In Erinnerung bleiben aber auch die großen Skandale dieser Dekade. Der Wettfavorit für das Derby von 1958, Alcide, wurde in seinem Stall grausam verletzt und konnte nicht an den Start gehen. Obwohl die Attentäter nie dingfest gemacht wurden, machten viele skrupellose Buchmacher für die Tat verantwortlich. Auf dem europäischen Festland vollbrachte derweil Federico Tesio ein weiteres Wunder. Das italienische Genie ging als Züchter von Ribot – einem der besten Vollblutpferde aller Zeiten – in die Geschichte ein, obwohl er sein Geschöpf nie hat laufen sehen. Ribot gewann den Grand Prix de l'Arc de Triomphe zweimal mit vollendeter Leichtigkeit und blieb ein unbestrittener und ungeschlagener Champion.

C'est en 1953 que Gordon Richards fut anobli pour son action en faveur des courses hippiques. Quelques jours plus tard, sur Pinza, il remportait le Derby qui lui avait toujours échappé. En 1954, le nouveau prodige des hippodromes, Lester Piggott, commençait à marcher sur les traces de Sir Gordon Richards et gagnait cette même course en montant l'outsider Never Say Die. La prédilection et l'engagement de la famille royale pour les courses ne faiblirent pas. C'est donc Pall Mall, un cheval de la reine Elizabeth II, qui s'adjugeait le 2 000 Guinées en 1958 tandis que la reine mère eut moins de chance puisque Devon Loch, la monture qu'elle avait engagée dans le steeple-chase du Grand National en 1956, devait chuter mystérieusement lors du galop final, alors que la voie était pratiquement libre. Durant les années cinquante, les épreuves de saut connurent aussi des moments forts. Sir Ken, généralement considéré le plus grand spécialiste de tous les temps en la matière, enlevait trois fois d'affilée le Champion Hurdles. Hélas la décennie restera aussi dans les mémoires comme celle de toutes les combines. Alcide, grand favori du Derby de 1958, fut ainsi cruellement blessé dans son box et contraint de renoncer à la course. Même si l'on ne trouva jamais ses agresseurs, de forts soupçons pesaient sur certains bookmakers malhonnêtes. En Europe continentale, Federico Tesio continuait de faire des merveilles. Bien qu'il n'ait jamais assisté à une seule course de Ribot, le génial Italien restera l'éleveur de l'un des meilleurs pur-sang de tous les temps. Ribot, champion hors pair invaincu et invincible, remporta avec brio le Grand Prix de l'Arc de Triomphe à deux reprises.

Youth takes on experience. Veteran
Gordon Richards on Denizen gives
fourteen-year-old Lester Piggott a
riding lesson at Lewes racecourse,
Sussex, 28 August 1950. The youthful
Piggott had many brushes with the
Stewards. His desire to win races by
going for narrow gaps became of deep
concern to the Jockey Club who
withdrew his jockey's licence because
of dangerous riding at Ascot in 1954.

Die Jugend sammelt Erfahrungen.
Altmeister Gordon Richards gibt
dem 14-jährigen Lester Piggott eine
Reitstunde auf der Lewes-Rennbahn
in Sussex, 28. August 1950. Der
jugendliche Piggott geriet oft mit
den Stewards aneinander. Seine Taktik,
während des Rennens in schmale
Lücken vorzustoßen, missfiel dem
Jockey Club, der ihm aufgrund
seines gefährlichen Stils 1954 in
Ascot die Reitlizenz entzog.

Les jeunes font leurs classes. Le vétéran
Gordon Richards donne à Lester Piggott,
alors âgé de 14 ans, une leçon de monte
sur l'hippodrome de Lewes, dans le
Sussex, 28 août 1950. Le jeune Piggott
eut bien des problèmes avec les organisateurs de courses. Sa soif de victoires
l'amenait à emprunter en course des
couloirs très étroits, au grand dam du
Jockey Club qui lui retira sa licence de
jockey pour comportement dangereux
à Ascot en 1954.

Cross-Channel raider.
Marcel Boussac,
looking as miserable
as usual, and a
happier jockey
Rae Johnstone,
after Galcador's
Derby win, 1950.

Siegreich jenseits
des Ärmelkanals.
Marcel Boussac, der
wie immer traurig
dreinblickt, und der
fröhlichere Jockey
Rae Johnstone nach
Galcadors Derby-
Gewinn im Jahre
1950.

Des conquérants
venus du continent.
Marcel Boussac fait
grise mine, comme à
l'accoutumée, à la
différence du jockey
Rae Johnstone qui
vient de remporter
le Derby de 1950
sur Galcador.

Up from Down Under. Top Australian jockey Rae Johnstone,
like so many of his fellow countrymen, an excellent judge of pace,
scores on Templier at Saint-Cloud, Paris, September 1950.

Vom fünften Kontinent an die Spitze. Der australische Top-Jockey
Rae Johnstone, wie viele seiner Landsmänner ein ausgezeichneter
Tempomacher, punktet auf Templier in Saint-Cloud, Paris, im
September 1950.

Tout droit venu d'Australie. Le jockey australien Rae Johnstone,
tout comme nombre de ses compatriotes, s'y connaît en matière
de rythme et mène Templier à la victoire à Saint-Cloud (Paris),
en septembre 1950.

Weightwatchers.
(Opposite)
Rae Johnstone
waits to weigh-in
at Saint-Cloud,
September 1950.
Another skilful
Australian,
Scobie Breasley,
wins his own weight
in sultanas from his
native land,
16 November 1959.

Weightwatchers.
(Gegenüber)
Rae Johnstone
wartet nach einem
Rennen in Saint-Cloud
darauf, gewogen zu
werden, September
1950. Ein anderer
Profi aus Australien,
Scobie Breasley,
gewinnt am
16. November 1959
sein eigenes Gewicht
in Rosinen aus
seinem Geburtsland.

Surveillez votre
poids! (Ci-contre)
Rae Johnstone,
attend d'être pesé
après la course de
Saint-Cloud, en sep-
tembre 1950.
Scobie Breasley, autre
Australien talentueux,
gagne son poids en
raisins provenant de
son pays natal,
16 novembre 1959.

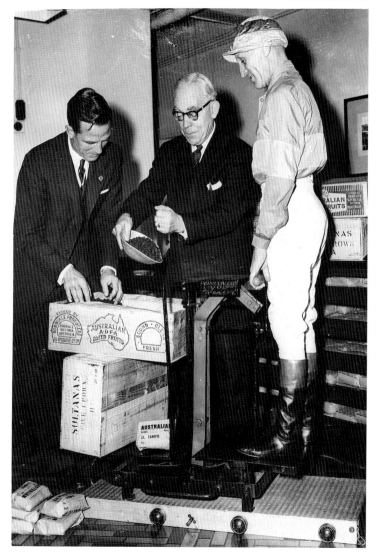

(Above, right) Sweating off. Royal jockey Harry Carr in the sweatbox at his Newmarket home, 27 February 1959. The picture on the wall above shows the Victorian champion jockey Fred Archer, who committed suicide due to depression caused by constant wasting. (Above, left) Relaxing under the heat lamp with a good book to pass the time.

(Oben rechts) Ausschwitzen. Der königliche Jockey Harry Carr im heimischen Schwitzkasten in Newmarket, 27. Februar 1959. Das Bild über ihm zeigt den Jockey Fred Archer, einen Champion aus der viktorianischen Zeit. Eine Depression, Folge ständiger Gewichtskontrollen, trieb Archer in den Selbstmord. (Oben links) Mit einem guten Buch unter der Hitzelampe entspannen.

(Ci-dessus, à droite) Éliminer. Harry Carr, le jockey de la famille royale, dans le caisson de transpiration de son domicile, à Newmarket, 27 février 1959. L'image fixée au mur représente le jockey de l'époque victorienne Fred Archer, qui se suicida à la suite d'une dépression nerveuse. (Ci-dessus, à gauche) Un peu de détente sous les lampes produisant de la chaleur, avec un bon livre pour passer le temps.

Stripping off. Jockey Manny Mercer, who sadly was killed in a fall at Ascot in 1959, removes a mud-splattered jacket after riding work on the Newmarket gallops, 1955.

Ausziehen. Jockey Manny Mercer, der 1959 den Tod bei einem unglücklichen Sturz in Ascot fand, zieht seine mit Schmutz bespritzte Jacke nach dem Training in Newmarket aus, 1955.

Mettez-vous à l'aise. Le jockey Manny Mercer, qui devait malheureusement trouver la mort lors d'une chute à Ascot en 1959, retire sa veste pleine de boue après une séance d'entraînement à Newmarket, 1955.

(Above) The first of many… Boy-wonder Lester Piggott on Never Say Die, the first of his nine Derby winners, 2 June 1954. (Opposite) Done it at last. Gordon Richards, recently knighted, wins his first Derby on Pinza, bred by his mentor, the now retired Fred Darling, 6 June 1953.

(Oben) Der erste von vielen Siegen. Wunderkind Lester Piggott mit Never Say Die, dem ersten seiner neun Derby-Sieger, am 2. Juni 1954. (Gegenüber) Endlich vollbracht. Gordon Richards, vor kurzem zum Ritter geschlagen, gewinnt am 6. Juni 1953 sein erstes Derby auf Pinza, der von seinem Mentor Fred Darling aufgezogen wurde.

(Ci-dessus) La première d'une longue série. Le prodige des courses, Lester Piggott, sur Never Say Die, remporte la première de ses neuf victoires du Derby, le 2 juin 1954. (Ci-contre) Enfin vainqueur. Gordon Richards, qui vient d'être anobli, enlève son premier Derby sur Pinza, élevé par son mentor Fred Darling, retiré du monde des courses, 6 juin 1953.

(Above) A Winter's Tale. Fred Winter keeps out the cold at Windsor, 1 March 1956. (Right) Schooldays. Former champion jump jockey Bryan Marshall, now a trainer, schooling a young stable inmate over hurdles, 4 September 1954.

(Oben) Ein Winter-Märchen. Fred Winter, gewappnet gegen die Kälte in Windsor, am 1. März 1956. (Rechts) Schultage. Der Trainer und ehemalige Hindernis-Champion Bryan Marshall übt mit einem jungen Pferd aus seinem Stall das Hindernisrennen, 4. September 1954.

(Ci-dessus) Conte d'hiver. Fred Winter (« hiver » en anglais) se protège du froid à Windsor, en ce 1er mars 1956. (À droite) À l'école. Le jockey Bryan Marshall, ancien champion des courses d'obstacles devenu entraîneur, enseigne le saut de haies à un jeune pensionnaire, 4 septembre 1954.

(Opposite) Habit forming. Royal Tan gives Bryan Marshall, trainer Vincent O'Brien and (right) owner Joe Griffin their second successive National, 27 March 1954. (Above) Standing to attention. Michael Scudamore, father of future jump champion jockey, Peter, and National winner Oxo, a former point-to-pointer, at the last, 21 March 1959.

(Gegenüber) Aus Gewohnheit. Royal Tan schenkt Bryan Marshall, Trainer Vincent O'Brien und Besitzer Joe Griffin (rechts) den zweiten Sieg in Folge bei der Grand National, 2. März 1954. In Hab-Acht-Stellung. Michael Scudamore, Vater von Peter, dem zukünftigen Champion-Jockey im Hindernisrennen, mit Oxo, ehemaliges Geländejagdpferd und Sieger in der Grand National am letzten Hindernis, 21 März 1959.

(Ci-contre) On prend des habitudes. Royal Tan offre sa deuxième victoire consécutive au Grand National à Bryan Marshall, à son entraîneur Vincent O'Brien et à son propriétaire Joe Griffin (à droite). Se mettre au garde-à-vous. Michael Scudamore, père du future champion de steeple-chase, Peter, sur Oxo, gagnant du Grand National, au dernier obstacle, 21 mars 1959.

Bathing beauties. Sunbathers at a swimming pool in Molesey, Surrey, get a grandstand
view of the start at Hurst Park, 26 July 1957. The popular metropolitan track, near
Hampton Court, which used to stage the top race, the Triumph Hurdle, closed soon after.

Badende Schönheiten. Die Sonnenanbeterinnen in einem Schwimmbad in Molesey, Surrey,
haben einen Haupttribünen-Blick auf den Start des Rennens in Hurst Park, 26. Juli 1957.
Die beliebte Rennstrecke nahe Hampton Court, auf der auch der Triumph Hurdle, ein erst-
klassiges Rennen, ausgetragen wurde, wurde kurze Zeit später geschlossen.

Beautés au bain. Les baigneuses d'une piscine de Molesey, dans le Surrey, sont aux premières
loges pour le départ de cette course à Hurst Park, 26 juillet 1957. Cet hippodrome populaire
et urbain, situé près d'Hampton Court, accueillait traditionnellement le Triumph Hurdle,
reine des épreuves et fut fermé peu de temps après.

Let it snow, let it snow, let it snow... A string of racehorses, trained by Captain Charles Elsey, walk through heavy snow after morning exercise at Malton, Yorkshire, 27 February 1954. Captain Elsey was the leading northern flat trainer for many years and sent out six Classic winners from his Highfield stables in the Forties and Fifties.

Lass es schneien... Eine Gruppe von Rennpferden, die von Captain Charles Elsey trainiert werden, trabt nach dem morgendlichen Training in Malton, Yorkshire, durch den Schnee, 27. Februar 1954. Captain Elsey war viele Jahre lang der führende Trainer für Flachrennen im Norden. In den vierziger und fünfziger Jahren kamen sechs Sieger klassischer Rennen aus seinen Ställen in Highfield.

Tombe la neige... Une colonne de chevaux de course, sous l'égide du capitaine Charles Elsey, foule un sol recouvert de neige après l'entraînement matinal à Malton, dans le Yorkshire, 27 février 1954. Dans le nord, le capitaine Elsey s'imposa comme le principal entraîneur de plat pendant de nombreuses années, les chevaux de ses écuries de Highfield remportant six classiques dans les années quarante et cinquante.

A religious experience. A glorious spring afternoon at Lincoln's packed racecourse. The city's famous cathedral, in ethereal splendour, looks down on the scene. Lester Piggott, always in the news it seemed, lost his licence for two months for preventing a hot favourite, Ione, from winning at Lincoln in the early Sixties.

Eine religiöse Erfahrung. Ein herrlicher Frühlingsnachmittag auf der überfüllten Rennbahn in Lincoln. Die berühmte Kathedrale der Stadt in ihrer zeitlosen Schönheit überragt die Szenerie. Lester Piggott, der ständig für Schlagzeilen sorgte, verlor in den frühen 60er Jahren für zwei Monate seine Lizenz, weil er den Top-Favoriten Ione am Sieg in Lincoln hinderte.

Une sorte de communion. Une belle après-midi de printemps sur l'hippodrome bondé de Lincoln. La célèbre cathédrale de la ville, à l'horizon, resplendissant d'un éclat irréel, surplombe la scène. Lester Piggott, qui semble devoir constamment défrayer la chronique, se vit retirer sa licence de jockey pour deux mois, pour avoir empêché Ione, l'un des favoris de la course, de l'emporter à Lincoln au début des années soixante.

(Above) An Italian stallion. The incredible Ribot and rider Enrico Camici win the King George VI and Queen Elizabeth Stakes at Ascot, 21 July 1956. (Opposite) The unbeaten Ribot at exercise at Ascot, 17 July 1956. Ribot only raced three times outside his native Italy, but still managed to win two Arc de Triomphes and the great Ascot race.

(Oben) Ein italienischer Hengst. Der unvergleichliche Ribot und Jockey Enrico Camici gewinnen die King George VI. and Queen Elizabeth Stakes von Ascot am 21. Juli 1956. (Gegenüber) Der ungeschlagene Ribot beim Training in Ascot am 17. Juli 1956. Ribot nahm nur an drei Rennen teil, die nicht in seinem Geburtsland Italien stattfanden. Er gewann zweimal den Grand Prix de l'Arc de Triomphe und einmal das große Rennen von Ascot.

(Ci-dessus) Un étalon italien. Le phénoménal Ribot et son cavalier Enrico Camici remportent le Prix du roi George VI et de la reine Elizabeth à Ascot, le 21 juillet 1956. (Ci-contre) Ribot, le champion invaincu, s'entraîne à Ascot, 17 juillet 1956. Ribot n'a participé qu'à trois courses en dehors de son Italie natale, remportant le Grand Prix de l'Arc de Triomphe à deux reprises et une fois le célèbre Prix d'Ascot.

Blonde bombshell. Cecilia Austin watches the Stewards' Cup from Trundle Hill high above Goodwood racecourse, 1953. Her attire shows that Goodwood rivals Ascot in the fashion stakes.

Blonde „Granate". Cecilia Austin beobachtet den Steward's Cup vom Trundle Hill aus, hoch über der Goodwood-Rennstrecke, 1953. Ihre Erscheinung beweist, dass Goodwood es in Sachen Mode durchaus mit Ascot aufnehmen kann.

Une blonde explosive. Cecilia Austin suit la Stewards' Cup du haut de Trundle Hill, la colline surplombant l'hippodrome de Goodwood, 1953. Les habits montrent que la mode affichée à Goodwood n'avait rien à envier à celle de l'hippodrome d'Ascot.

Summer holiday. The finish of the Trundle Handicap at Glorious Goodwood, the idyllic course on the Sussex Downs. Harry Lime is the winner, 29 July 1954. Not every horse acts on Goodwood's tight turns and undulations. Over the years punters have learnt to follow horses with previous form over the unique and demanding track.

Sommerferien. Das Finish im Trundle Handicap von Glorious Goodwood, der idyllischen Strecke zwischen den Hügeln von Sussex. Der Sieger an diesem 29. Juli 1954 hieß Harry Lime. Nicht alle Pferde kommen mit den engen Kurven und der welligen Strecke von Goodwood gut zurecht. Daher sind die Wetter mit der Zeit dazu übergegangen, auf Pferde zu setzen, die bei früheren Starts auf diesem sehr anspruchsvollen Kurs bereits ihre Kapazitäten unter Beweis gestellt hatten.

Vacances d'été. Arrivée à Glorious Goodwood du handicap Trundle, la somptueuse course des collines du Sussex. Harry Lime enlève cette épreuve, 29 juillet 1954. Tous les chevaux ne se sentent pas forcément à l'aise en raison des virages serrés et des ondulations du terrain. Au fil des ans, les parieurs ont appris à faire confiance aux chevaux qui se sont déjà illustrés sur cette piste unique en son genre et fort périlleuse.

Return of the native. (Above) American owner Alfred G Vanderbilt with his champion Native Dancer, Eric Guerin up, after a Belmont Park two-year-old victory, 14 September 1952. Native Dancer won two legs of the American Triple Crown as a three-year-old the following year. (Opposite) Vanderbilt and his wife Jean Murray.

Rückkehr. (Oben) Der amerikanische Pferdebesitzer Alfred G. Vanderbilt mit seinem Champion Native Dancer und Jockey Eric Guerin nach ihrem Sieg bei einem Rennen für Zweijährige in Belmont Park am 14. September 1952. Im folgenden Jahr konnte das Pferd als Dreijähriges zwei Konkurrenzen der amerikanischen Triple Crown gewinnen. (Gegenüber) Vanderbilt und seine Frau Jean Murray.

Retour triomphal. (Ci-dessus) Le propriétaire américain Alfred G. Vanderbilt et le champion Native Dancer, monté par Eric Guérin, après leur victoire à Belmont Park dans une course pour les chevaux de deux ans, 14 septembre 1952. Dans la catégorie des chevaux de trois ans, Native Dancer remportait l'année suivante deux des manches de la triple couronne américaine. (Ci-contre) Vanderbilt et son épouse Jean Murray.

All together now. Even the judge can't split them. A triple dead-heat in Melbourne, 6 November 1956. In 1923 this rare occurrence happened at a British racecourse – Windsor. It was even stranger that one of the jockeys, Gardner, had been involved in a triple dead-heat at Sandown Park eight years earlier.

Alle zugleich. Selbst der Zielrichter konnte bei diesem toten Rennen mit drei zeitgleichen Pferden in Melbourne keinen Sieger ausmachen, 6. November 1956. Im Jahre 1923 hatte es dieses seltene Ereignis auf der britischen Rennbahn von Windsor schon einmal gegeben. Noch seltsamer war der Umstand, dass mit Gardner einer der drei zeitgleichen Jockeys bereits acht Jahre zuvor in Sandown Park ein „dreifach totes Rennen" lief.

Tous ensemble. Même le juge n'est pas en mesure de les départager. Ces trois chevaux sont ex-æquo lors d'une course à Melbourne, 6 novembre 1956. Fait rarissime, le cas s'était déjà présenté en Grande-Bretagne, lors d'une course à Windsor en 1923. Encore plus étrange : l'un des jockeys concernés, Gardner, avait été impliqué dans une triple égalité huit ans plus tôt à Sandown Park.

Silent movie. Smiling film star Hedy Lamarr and a flower-bedecked Da Dawn, the winner of a charity day race at Santa Anita racetrack, Los Angeles, California, 19 January 1950. The city has two racecourses, Santa Anita and Hollywood Park, but racing moves to Del Mar, San Diego, in summer, when the heat becomes too oppressive in the city.

Stummfilm. Der lächelnde Filmstar Hedy Lamarr und ein mit Blumen geschmückter Da Dawn, Sieger bei einem Benefizrennen auf der Santa-Anita-Rennbahn in Los Angeles, Kalifornien, 19. Januar 1950. Los Angeles verfügt mit Santa Anita und Hollywood Park über zwei Rennbahnen. Die Rennen finden im Hochsommer jedoch, wenn die Hitze in der Stadt unerträglich wird, in Del Mar, San Diego, statt.

Un film muet. La vedette de cinéma Hedy Lamarr, tout sourire, accompagne Da Dawn couvert de fleurs, après sa victoire lors d'une course de charité à l'hippodrome de Santa Anita, dans la ville de Los Angeles, en Californie, 19 janvier 1950. Il y a deux hippodromes à Los Angeles : celui de Santa Anita et celui d'Hollywood Park. Mais lorsqu'en été la chaleur devient trop accablante, les courses se déroulent sur le champ de courses de Del Mar, à San Diego.

Kings and queens. (Above) Triple Champion Hurdle winner Sir Ken (number 3) and Tim Molony at Cheltenham, 3 March 1953. Sir Ken was trained by Willie Stephenson who had a golden spell in the Fifties, winning the Derby with Arctic Prince and the Grand National with Oxo. (Opposite) Her Majesty Queen Elizabeth II leads in her Oaks winner Carrozza, with Lester Piggott up, June 1957.

Könige und Königinnen. (Oben) Der dreifache Champion-Hurdle-Sieger Sir Ken (Nummer 3) und Jockey Tim Molony in Cheltenham am 3. März 1953. Sir Ken wurde von Willie Stephenson trainiert. Stephenson holte in den Fünfzigern das Derby mit Arctic Prince und gewann mit Oxo die Grand National. (Gegenüber) Ihre Majestät Queen Elizabeth II. präsentiert ihr Pferd Carrozza mit Jockey Lester Piggott nach ihrem Sieg bei den Oaks im Juni 1957.

Rois et reines. (Ci-dessus) Le triple vainqueur du Champion Hurdle Sir Ken (numéro 3) et Tim Molony à Cheltenham, 3 mars 1953. Sir Ken était entraîné par Willie Stephenson, qui connut une période faste dans les années cinquante, remportant le Derby avec Arctic Prince et le Grand national avec Oxo. (Ci-contre) Sa Majesté la reine Elizabeth II conduit son cheval Carrozza, vainqueur des Oaks et monté ici par Lester Piggott, en juin 1957.

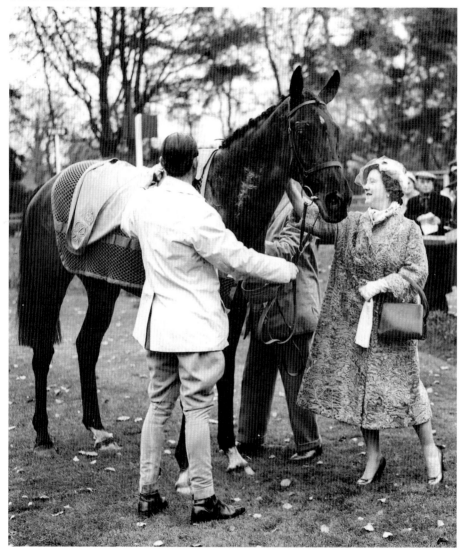

(Opposite) Mothers'
Day. Her Majesty
the Queen Mother
pats Double Star at
Sandown Park,
21 November 1958.
(Right) Fathers' Day.
Prince Aly Khan with
his father's Derby
hero Tulyar and
Charlie Smirke,
19 June 1952.

(Gegenüber) Mutter-
tag. Ihre Majestät
die Königinmutter
gibt Double Star
einen Klaps,
Sandown Park,
21. November 1958.
(Rechts) Vatertag.
Der Prinz Aly Khan
mit Jockey Charlie
Smirke auf Tulyar,
dem heldenhaften
Derby-Sieger aus dem
Besitz seines Vaters,
am 19. Juni 1952.

(Ci-contre) La fête
des Mères. Sa
Majesté la reine
mère caresse Double
Star à Sandown Park,
le 21 novembre 1958.
(À droite) La fête des
Pères. Le Prince Aly
Khan avec Tulyar, le
héros du Derby monté
par Charlie Smirke,
le 19 juin 1952.

Monarchic mayhem. The Queen Mother's Devon Loch (number 5) and Dick Francis at Becher's. Later unlucky Devon Loch, who would have won the National with ease, did the splits when well clear on the run in, March 1956.

Königliches Waterloo. Devon Loch, das Pferd der Königinmutter (Nummer 5), mit Jockey Dick Francis am Hindernis Becher's Brook bei der Grand National im März 1956. Das unglückselige Pferd vergab den sicheren Sieg trotz großen Vorsprungs, als es auf der Zielgeraden in den Spagat ging und stürzte.

Un désordre monarchique. Devon Loch (numéro 5), le cheval de la reine mère et Dick Francis franchissant la haie à Becher's. Par la suite, Devon Loch, qui aurait dû remporter le Grand National haut la main, fit le grand écart alors que la voie était libre vers la victoire, mars 1956.

(Left) Devon Loch about to collapse. (Below, left) A disbelieving Dick Francis. (Below, right) The Queen and the Queen Mother shelter in the paddock.

(Links) Devon Loch kurz vor dem Sturz. (Links unten) Der völlig ungläubige Dick Francis. (Rechts unten) Die Queen und ihre Mutter ziehen sich auf die Koppel und unter ihre Regenschirme zurück.

(À gauche) Devon Loch est sur le point de tomber. (Ci-dessous, à gauche) Dick Francis n'en croit pas ses yeux. (Ci-dessous, à droite) La reine et la reine mère s'abritent dans le paddock.

National nutcracker. An anxious moment for the eventual winner, Teal (far left, spotted colours) and Arthur Thompson at the first fence in the National, 5 April 1952. Teal was trained in Middleham, North Yorkshire, by Captain Neville Crump, who also won the National with Sheila's Cottage and Merryman II.

Eine harte Nuss. Ein kritischer Moment für den späteren Grand-National-Sieger Teal und Jockey Arthur Thompson (ganz links, im gepunkteten Dress) am ersten Hindernis des Rennens, 5. April 1952. Teal wurde in Middleham, North Yorkshire, von Captain Neville Crump trainiert, der mit Sheila's Cottage und Merryman II zwei weitere Gewinner der Grand National betreute.

Hécatombe au Grand National. Moment d'angoisse pour Teal, le vainqueur final (casaque à pois, tout à gauche) et Arthur Thompson sur cette première haie du National, 5 avril 1952. Teal était entraîné à Middleham, dans le nord du Yorkshire, par le Capitaine Neville Crump qui enleva aussi le National avec Sheila's Cottage et Merryman II.

Jockey and mount come crashing down to earth as Alan Honeybone takes a heavy tumble from
El Griego II at Sandown, 19 January 1957. Sandown's notoriously difficult railway fences, which are
positioned close together on the far side of the track, present the ultimate test for a steeplechaser
and its rider.

Ross El Griego II und Reiter Alan Honeybone machen auf unsanfte Weise Bekanntschaft mit dem Geläuf
von Sandown, 19. Januar 1957. Die berüchtigten, direkt an den Zuschauertribünen positionierten, kurz
aufeinander folgenden Hindernisse von Sandown sind die ultimative Herausforderung für Pferd und Reiter.

Le jockey et sa monture s'écrasent au sol. À Sandown, Alan Honeybone chute lourdement de son cheval
El Griego II, 19 janvier 1957. Les haies barrés de Sandown, proches l'une de l'autre et positionnées à
l'endroit le plus éloignée de la piste, sont réputées pour leur difficulté et constituent le test de référence
pour les spécialistes du steeple-chase et leurs jockeys.

Cutting up the turf as they speed into the distance at the British flat season's last big race, the Manchester November Handicap, at Castle Irwell, 17 November 1951. Manchester closed in 1964 and this race moved to Doncaster.

Umgepflügter Turf beim letzten großen Rennen der britischen Flach-renn-Saison, dem Manchester November Handicap in Castle Irwell, 17. November 1951. 1964 wurde der Rennbetrieb in Manchester einge-stellt. Das Rennen wechselte nach Doncaster.

Les concurrents la-bourent la piste alors qu'ils s'élancent pour la dernière grande course de la saison de plat britannique, le Handicap de Novem-bre à Manchester, couru au Castle Irwell, 17 novembre 1951. L'hippodrome de Manchester fut fermé en 1964 et cette course fut dès lors disputée à Doncaster.

(Left) Parade of stars. The pre-race parade for the 1950 Derby. (Opposite) Brighton Belle. Persian Chariot and Brian Jago score at Brighton, a down-hill track that closely resembles Epsom, 4 August 1959.

(Links) Einmarsch der Helden. Die Parade vor dem Derby von 1950. (Gegenüber) Die Schönen von Brighton. Persian Chariot und Brian Jago punkten am 4. August 1959 in Brighton. Die ab-schüssige Bahn von Brighton ähnelt der Strecke von Epsom.

(À gauche) Le défilé des stars. Défilé des concurrents avant le Derby de 1950. (Ci-contre) Brighton Belle. Persian Chariot et Brian Jago se placent à Brighton, dont la piste en pente ressemble beaucoup à celle d'Epsom, 4 août 1959.

(Above) Head over heels. Amateur rider
Captain T Muir takes a purler at Sandown,
14 March 1952. (Left) Roll with it. Future
champion jump jockey Josh Gifford and mount
come an ungainly cropper in full view of the
cameras at Hurst Park, 18 December 1957.

(Oben) Hals über Kopf. Ein schwerer Sturz des
Amateur-Jockeys Captain T. Muir in Sandown am
14. März 1952. (Links) Rolle rückwärts. Der
spätere Champion-Jockey im Hindernisrennen
Josh Gifford und sein Pferd posieren nicht ganz
freiwillig und reichlich unvorteilhaft für die
Kameras in Hurst Park, 18. Dezember 1957.

(Ci-dessus) Les quatre fers en l'air. Le Capitaine
T. Muir, jockey amateur, fait une chute ren-
versante à Sandown, le 14 mars 1952.
(À gauche) Roulé-boulé. Josh Gifford, futur
champion de saut, et sa monture chutent
malencontreusement sous l'œil des photographes
à Hurst Park, le 18 décembre 1957.

(Left) Trainer Harry Wragg, May 1950.
(Opposite, above) Peter Robinson picks up the pace in Wragg's covered ride, 15 October 1955.
(Opposite, below) Wragg's head lad Harry Constable watches horses exercising, 13 March 1954.

(Links) Der Trainer Harry Wragg im Mai 1950.
(Gegenüber, oben) Peter Robinson auf Wraggs überdachtem Reitweg, 15. Oktober 1955.
(Gegenüber, unten) Wraggs Chef-Stallbursche Harry Constable beobachtet eine Reihe trainierender Pferde, 13. März 1954.

(À gauche) L'entraîneur Harry Wragg en mai 1950.
(Ci-contre, en haut) Peter Robinson en rhythme sur la piste couverte de Wragg, 15 octobre 1955.
(Ci-contre, en bas) Le chef des écuries, Harry Constable, observe une file de chevaux à l'entraînement, 13 mars 1954.

6. Ringing the changes
Die Dinge ändern sich
L'heure des bouleversements

French kiss. Mud-spattered jockey Max Garcia plants a kiss on the nose of an equally muddy Puissant Chef after winning the Prix de l'Arc de Triomphe at Longchamp, Paris. Owner Henri Aubert reflects upon his success, 9 October 1960. Puissant Chef was trained by Mick Bartholomew, a member of the famous Anglo-French training family.

Französische Küsse. Der mit Schlamm bespritzte Jockey Max Garcia küsst die Nüstern des gleichermaßen dreckigen Puissant Chef nach ihrem Sieg beim Grand Prix de l'Arc de Triomphe in Longchamp, 9. Oktober 1960. Der nachdenkliche Eigentümer des Pferdes, Henri Aubert, steht links. Puissant Chefs Trainer war Mick Bartholomew, Mitglied einer bekannten anglo-französischen Handelsfamilie.

Un baiser. Max Garcia, le visage maculé de boue embrasse le museau tout aussi crotté de Puissant Chef après leur victoire dans le Grand Prix de l'Arc de Triomphe à Longchamp (Paris), 9 octobre 1960. Le propriétaire Henri Aubert semble méditer son succès. Puissant Chef était entraîné par Mick Bartholomew, représentant de la célèbre famille franco-anglaise des entraîneurs.

The Swinging Sixties invented the mini-skirt and spawned the permissive society. Although changes in the sport were less momentous, racing also moved with the times. Camera patrols and starting stalls appeared on British racecourses. The betting shop arrived on Britain's high streets. There were titanic duels between Arkle and Mill House over jumps; Fred Winter somehow steered Mandarin to victory in the 1962 Grand Steeplechase de Paris, despite having a broken bit. There were equally exhilarating performances on the flat: the French-trained Sea Bird II cruised home in effortless style in the 1965 Derby and the Arc de Triomphe. Sheer class and a vintage ride from Lester Piggott propelled the brave Sir Ivor, who barely stayed a mile and a half, to win at Epsom in 1968. Northern Dancer, later, at stud, to be the world's most sought after stallion, raised the profile of Canadian racing to new heights. Argentina's Forli and South Africa's Hawaii also proved that champions can emerge from the unlikeliest of backgrounds. Although breeding purists found it hard to digest, the greatest crowd puller of the age was the gelding Kelso. Voted Horse of the Year an incredible five times, Kelso drew a staggering 71,000 people to Aqueduct on Labor Day 1963 to cheer their hero home.

Die „Swinging Sixties" brachten den Minirock und die freizügige Gesellschaft. Obwohl sich die gesellschaftlichen Veränderungen kaum auf den Pferdesport auswirkten, ging dieser doch mit der Zeit. Kameras und Startboxen hielten Einzug auf den britischen Rennbahnen. In den Einkaufsstraßen wurden Wettbüros allgegenwärtig. Arkle und Mill House lieferten sich unsterbliche Duelle beim Hindernisrennen. Trotz einer gebrochenen Gebiss-Stange gelang es Fred Winter auf wundersame Weise, sein Pferd Mandarin im Hindernisrennen beim Grand Steeplechase de Paris des Jahres 1962 zum Sieg zu führen. Ähnlich atemberaubende Vorstellungen hatte das Flachrennen zu bieten: Das in Frankreich trainierte Pferd Sea Bird II gewann 1965 in seinem mühelosen Stil beim Derby und im Grand Prix de l'Arc de Triomphe. Pure Klasse und ein herausragender Ritt von Lester Piggott verhalfen dem tapferen Sir Ivor – der kaum je anderthalb Meilen durchhielt – 1968 zu einem großen Sieg in Epsom. Northern Dancer bescherte dem kanadischen Pferderennsport ein großes Ansehen. Später wurde er zum begehrtesten Hengst von Gestüten weltweit. Forli aus Argentinien und das südafrikanische Pferd Hawaii stellten zudem unter Beweis, dass auch die entlegensten

Herkunftsorte große Champions hervorbringen können. Obwohl Zucht-Puristen ein Dorn im Auge, war der Wallach Kelso der größte Publikumsmagnet dieser Zeit. Kelso wurde unglaubliche fünf Mal zum Pferd des Jahres gewählt und zog am Tag der Arbeit 1963 sage und schreibe 71 000 Zuschauer im Aqueduct-Rennen an, die ihren Held bejubelten.

Les années soixante virent l'apparition des premières minijupes et la libération des mœurs. Même si le monde des courses fut loin de connaître des bouleversements révolutionnaires, une vague d'innovations déferla sur les hippodromes. Ainsi furent installées des caméras mobiles et des stalles de départ sur les champs de courses britanniques. Dans les rues commerçantes, les officines de paris devenaient omniprésentes. Sur les obstacles, des duels titanesques opposaient Arkle et Mill House. En 1962, au Grand Steeple-Chase de Paris, Fred Winter conduisait Mandarin à la victoire malgré une rupture du mors. Sur le plat, les performances réalisées n'étaient pas moins passionnantes. Sea Bird II, dont l'entraîneur était français, remportait dans un style décontracté le Derby et l'Arc de Triomphe en 1965. La perfection de Lester Piggott ainsi que son style de monte à l'ancienne permirent au courageux Sir Ivor, qui tenait difficilement les 2 400m, de trouver les ressources suffisantes pour remporter le Grand Prix d'Epsom en 1968. Northern Dancer, qui allait devenir l'étalon le plus convoité, ouvrit de nouvelles perspectives au monde canadien des courses. De leur côté, les chevaux argentins Forli et Sud-Africain Hawaii démontrèrent que les champions pouvaient avoir les origines les plus douteuses. Et même si, parmi les éleveurs, les puristes trouvèrent la pilule un peu dure à avaler, le hongre Kelso fut bel et bien le cheval le plus populaire de l'époque. Consacré à cinq reprises Cheval de l'Année, il fut accueilli en héros par une foule de 71 000 personnes à son retour à Aqueduct le 1er mai 1963.

Dancing in time. (Above) Canada's Northern Dancer and groom. (Right) Jockey Bill Hartack and Northern Dancer, the winner of the Kentucky Derby, 1964. Northern Dancer later became the best stallion of all time and was the sire of the Derby winners Nijinsky, The Minstrel and Secreto.

Auf zum Tanz. (Oben) Der kanadische Northern Dancer mit einem Stallburschen. (Rechts) Northern Dancer und Jockey Bill Hartack nach ihrem Sieg beim 1964er Kentucky Derby. Nach seiner Rennkarriere wurde Northern Dancer zum erfolgreichsten Deckhengst aller Zeiten: Er zeugte die Derby-Sieger Nijinsky, The Minstrel und Secreto.

En rythme. (Ci-dessus) Le cheval canadien Northern Dancer et son lad. (À droite) Le jockey Bill Hartack et Northern Dancer, vainqueur du Derby du Kentucky en 1964. Northern Dancer devint par la suite le meilleur étalon de tous les temps et le géniteur de vainqueurs du Derby, tels que Nijinsky, The Minstrel et Secreto.

Prize-giving. A victorious lady owner receives an elegant silver elephant trophy from a race sponsor, 24 April 1961. The winning jockey looks more interested in the bottles of beer on the table. Riding a finish on a hot summer day is always thirsty work…

Preisverleihung. Eine siegreiche Pferdebesitzerin nimmt die elegante Elefanten-Trophäe aus den Händen eines Rennsponsors entgegen, 24. April 1961. Der siegreiche Jockey scheint sich mehr für das Bier auf dem Tisch zu interessieren. Das Finish an einem heißen Sommertag zu reiten, macht schließlich durstig…

Remise de prix. La gagnante d'une statuette d'éléphant en argent se voit décerner le prix de la part du sponsor de la course, 24 avril 1961. Le jockey ayant remporté la course semble plus attiré par les bouteilles de bière sur la table. Les courses disputées par de chaudes journées d'été donnent toujours soif…

Thanks, Ma'am. Terry Biddlecombe shares a joke with the Queen Mother as she presents the champion jump jockey with a horse's head memento for winning the Mackeson Gold Cup at Cheltenham on Gay Trip, November 1969. Biddlecombe was unfortunately injured when Gay Trip won the National a year later. Pat Taaffe was an able deputy.

Danke Ma'am. Die Königinmutter und Hindernis-Champion Terry Biddlecombe haben sichtlich Spaß bei der Verleihung dieser Pferdekopf-Miniatur anlässlich Biddlecombes Sieg im Mackeson Gold Cup. Der Jockey gewann das Rennen in Cheltenham im November 1969 auf Gay Trip. Als das Pferd im darauf folgenden Jahr die Grand National gewann, musste Biddlecombe leider verletzt zuschauen. Pat Taaffe war jedoch ein würdiger Ersatz.

Merci M'dam. Terry Biddlecombe plaisante avec la reine mère qui remet au champion des courses d'obstacles le trophée (une tête de cheval) récompensant le vainqueur de la Mackeson Gold Cup à Cheltenham sur Gay Trip, en novembre 1969. Biddlecombe était malheureusement blessé lorsque Gay Trip remporta le National l'année suivante et Pat Taaffe se révéla un digne remplaçant.

Saint Yves. The top French jockey Yves Saint-Martin, with Nelcius, the winner of the Prix du Jockey Club, at Chantilly, 6 June 1966. Although Nelcius was trained by Miguel Clement, most of Saint-Martin's big race successes were provided by François Mathet, the doyen of French trainers.

Heiliger Yves. Der französische Spitzen-Jockey Yves Saint-Martin mit Nelcius nach seinem Sieg beim Prix du Jockey Club in Chantilly am 6. Juni 1966. Nelcius wurde von Miguel Clement trainiert. Die Mehrzahl seiner Erfolge jedoch feierte Saint-Martin mit Pferden aus der Ägide des Altmeisters der französischen Trainer, François Mathet.

St Yves. Le champion français Yves Saint-Martin et le cheval Nelcius remportent le Prix du Jockey Club à Chantilly, le 6 juin 1966. Nelcius était entraîné par Miguel Clement mais c'est à François Mathet, le doyen des entraîneurs français, que Saint-Martin doit ses plus grands succès.

Lotus-eater.
German Derby
winner Herero with
a piece of the
victory garland
between his teeth
at Hamburg race-
course. Amused and
contented jockey
Hein Bellow looks
on, 1 July 1962.

Lotus-Fresser.
Herero, Gewinner
im Deutschen Derby,
kostet auf der Renn-
bahn von Hamburg
den Siegerkranz.
Jockey Hein Bellow
schaut amüsiert
und zufrieden zu,
1. Juli 1962.

Plaisir de sybarite.
Herero, vainqueur du
Derby allemand, tient
la couronne de la vic-
toire entre ses dents
sur l'hippodrome de
Hambourg sous le
regard amusé et satis-
fait de Hein Bellow,
1er juillet 1962.

The greatest of them all. (Above) Sea Bird II and Pat Glennon win the Derby on a tight rein, 2 June 1965. (Opposite) Sea Bird II taking everything in his stride on Derby Day morning. Like Vaguely Noble, Sea Bird was trained by Etienne Pollet at Chantilly and also won the Arc de Triomphe.

Wahre Größe. (Oben) Pat Glennon hat die Zügel fest in der Hand und gewinnt mit Sea Bird II das Derby am 2. Juni 1965. (Gegenüber) Selbstbewusst und gemessenen Schrittes – Sea Bird II am Morgen des Derby-Tages. Genau wie Vaguely Noble, wurde das Pferd von Etienne Pollet in Chantilly trainiert und siegte ebenfalls beim Grand Prix de l'Arc de Triomphe.

Le plus grand. (Ci-dessus) Sea Bird II et Pat Glennon remportent le Derby, les rênes courtes, 2 juin 1965. (Ci-contre) Sea Bird II semble serein le matin du Derby. À l'instar de Vaguely Noble, Sea Bird était entraîné par Etienne Pollet à Chantilly et remporta également l'Arc de Triomphe.

(Opposite) Arkle, winner of three successive Cheltenham Gold Cups, after an Ascot win, 5 December 1964. (Above) Arkle (left) and Pat Taaffe on the way to a second Gold Cup. His rival, Mill House (Willie Robinson up), is able to match strides briefly, 11 March 1965. (Following spread) The 1965 National winner, the American horse Jay Trump, and rider, Tommy Smith, train at Fred Winter's Lambourn stable, 26 February 1965.

(Gegenüber) Arkle, das dreimal in Folge beim Cheltenham-Gold-Cup gewann, nach dem Sieg in Ascot, 5. Dezember 1964. (Oben) Arkle (links) mit Pat Taaffe auf dem Weg zum zweiten Gold-Cup-Sieg. Arkles Rivale Mill House (rechts, mit Willie Robinson) kann nur kurzzeitig folgen, 11 März 1965. (Folgende Doppelseite) Das amerikanische Pferd Jay Trump, Sieger bei der 1965er Grand National, und Tommy Smith beim Training bei Fred Winter in Lambourn, 26. Februar 1965.

(Ci-contre) Arkle, vainqueur trois fois de suite de la Cheltenham Gold Cup après une victoire à Ascot, le 5 décembre 1964. (Ci-dessus) Arkle (à gauche) et Pat Taaffe sont en route pour une seconde Gold Cup. Mill House, son rival monté ici par Willie Robinson lui tient brièvement tête, 11 mars 1965. (Pages suivantes) Jay Trump, le cheval américain, vainqueur du National en 1965 et Tommy Smith s'entraînent chez Fred Winter à Lambourn, 26 février 1965.

Moore's the better.
Australian jockey
George Moore
in the royal colours,
and trainer Noël
Murless in the New-
market paddock,
19 April 1967.

Alles roger, Moore?
Der australische
Jockey George
Moore im könig-
lichen Dress mit
Trainer Noël Murless
auf der Koppel in
Newmarket am
19. April 1967.

Moore est le meilleur.
Le jockey australien
George Moore
arborant les couleurs
royales se trouve ici
en compagnie de
l'entraîneur Noël
Murless dans le pad-
dock de Newmarket,
19 avril 1967.

Lots more. Moore pilots Fleet, the 1,000 Guineas winner, to another big race victory in Royal Ascot's Coronation Stakes, 21 June 1967. Moore had a splendid year in Britain, winning the Derby and the 2,000 Guineas on Royal Palace, who was also trained by Murless.

Moore dirigiert 1 000-Guineas-Sieger Fleet zu einem weiteren großen Triumph bei den Coronation Stakes von Royal Ascot, 21. Juni 1967. Moore verbrachte ein äußerst erfolgreiches Jahr in Großbritannien: Zum Derby-Gewinn gesellte sich der Sieg bei den 2 000 Guineas auf Royal Palace, ebenfalls trainiert von Noël Murless.

Et il le prouve! Moore monte Fleet, déjà vainqueur du 1 000 Guinées, pour une autre grande victoire dans le Royal Ascot's Coronation Stakes, 21 juin 1967. Moore fit une saison magnifique en Grande-Bretagne, enlevant le Derby et les 2 000 Guinées sur Royal Palace, également entraîné par Murless.

Winter sports. Groundsmen worked all night to clear snow from the track for the first race
meeting of the season at Bowie, Maryland, 14 January 1965. If Bowie had been a grass track,
like the majority of European racecourses, racing would certainly have been abandoned.

Wintersport. Nachdem die Platzwarte über Nacht das Gelände vom Schnee befreit hatten,
konnte das erste Meeting der Saison am 14. Januar 1965 in Bowie, Maryland, stattfinden. Im
Gegensatz zu den meisten europäischen Rennstrecken war Bowie keine Rasenbahn. Ansonsten
wäre das Rennen sicherlich abgesagt worden.

Sports d'hiver. Les employés de l'hippodrome ont travaillé toute la nuit afin de déblayer la neige
qui s'était accumulée sur la piste, avant le premier meeting de la saison à Bowie, dans le
Maryland, 14 janvier 1965. Si la piste avait été couverte d'herbe, comme dans la plupart des
hippodromes européens, la course aurait certainement été annulée.

Water sports.
A gallant gentleman
lifts a stranded lady
across a puddle on
the third day of a
rain-soaked Royal
Ascot, 18 June 1964.
Not surprisingly,
racing was called off
because the course
was waterlogged.

Wassersport.
Dieser zuvorkom-
mende Gentleman
hilft einer gestrande-
ten Lady über eine
Pfütze. Wir schreiben
den 18. Juni 1964,
der dritte Tag eines
verregneten Royal
Ascot. Keine Über-
raschung also, dass
an diesem Tag alle
Rennen auf der über-
schwemmten Bahn
abgesagt wurden.

Sports aquatiques.
Un galant homme
aide cette dame à
traverser une flaque
d'eau en ce troisième
jour d'un Royal
Ascot pluvieux,
18 juin 1964.
En toute logique les
courses furent
annulées, le terrain
étant impraticable.

Glorious vista. The old paddock at
Goodwood with Trundle Hill in the
background, 30 July 1968.

Herrliche Aussicht. Die alte Koppel von
Goodwood am 30. Juli 1968. Im Hintergrund sieht man Trundle Hill.

Un joli point de vue. L'ancien paddock
de Goodwood et Trundle Hill à l'arrière-
plan, 30 juillet 1968.

Knight in shining armour. The Vincent O'Brien-trained Sir Ivor gets a peach of a ride
from Lester Piggott to take the Derby, 29 May 1968. As Sir Ivor barely stayed the Derby
trip of a mile and a half, this was widely recognised as Piggott's cleverest Epsom win.

Ritter von der glänzenden Gestalt. Lester Piggotts makelloser Ritt führt den von Vincent
O'Brien trainierten Sir Ivor am 29. Mai 1968 zum Derby-Sieg. Da Sir Ivor die Strecke
von anderthalb Meilen für gewöhnlich kaum durchstand, galt Piggotts Sieg in Epsom als
der cleverste seiner Karriere.

Un chevalier dans son armure dorée. Sir Ivor, entraîné par Vincent O'Brien, est magnifiquement monté par Lester Piggott et remporte ce Derby, 29 mai 1968. Sir Ivor
tenait difficilement les 2 400 mètres du Derby et cette victoire fut considérée par tous
comme la plus habile de Piggott à Epsom.

'I could have been as good as Lester if only I'd had the chance.' A tipster in jockey's silks rides a mythical finish in front of a group of racegoers on Derby Day. The tipster was obviously a clairvoyant: he is wearing Sir Ivor's colours, June 1960.

„Ich wäre so gut wie Lester gewesen, hätte man mich nur gelassen." Ein Tippgeber im Jockey-Dress imitiert für die Zuschauer das Finish am Derby Day im Juni 1960. Der Mann war offenbar ein Hellseher – er trägt die Farben des späteren Siegers, Sir Ivor.

« Si on m'avait laissé ma chance, j'aurais pu être aussi bon que Lester. » Un parieur en tenue de jockey dispute une arrivée imaginaire devant un groupe d'amateurs de courses, un jour de Derby, juin 1960. Il a assurément un don de prédiction puisqu'il porte ici les couleurs de Sir Ivor.

(Above) Victory lap. Yves Saint-Martin and the 1963
Derby winner Relko. (Right) Leader of the pack. Scobie
Breasley, who was said to have a clock in his head and
won many races by waiting in front, and Malberry make
the running at Windsor, 21 September 1964.

(Oben) Ehrenrunde für Yves Saint-Martin und den
Derby-Sieger von 1963, Relko. (Rechts) Immer vorne-
weg. Scobie Breasley und Malberry (vorne) ziehen den
Sprint an, Windsor, 21. September 1964. Breasley
wurde nachgesagt, er habe ein Uhrwerk im Kopf, weil
er viele Rennen vom Start weg in Front liegend gewann.

(Ci-dessus) Le tour d'honneur. Yves Saint-Martin et
Relko, le vainqueur du Derby en 1963. (À droite) Scobie
Breasley, réputé pour sa régularité de métronome,
remporta de nombreuses épreuves en se mettant dès
le départ à la tête du peloton. Ici, Breasley et Malberry
mènent la course à Windsor, 21 septembre 1964.

Two-year-old colt Vaguely Noble is sold for a record 136,000 guineas at Newmarket's December Sales, 7 December 1967, to American plastic surgeon, Dr Robert Franklyn, who later saw his substantial investment increase in value.

Das zweijährige Fohlen Vaguely Noble wird bei der Auktion am 7. Dezember 1967 in Newmarket für die Rekordsumme von 136 000 Guineas an den amerikanischen Chirurgen Dr. Robert Franklyn verkauft. Eine lohnende Investition, wie sich herausstellen sollte.

Le poulain de deux ans, Vaguely Noble est vendu pour la somme record de 136 000 guinées lors des ventes de décembre à Newmarket, 7 décembre 1967. L'acheteur était le Dr Robert Franklyn, un spécialiste de la chirurgie plastique qui vit par la suite la valeur de son investissement s'accroître.

Money well spent. Vaguely Noble and Bill Williamson easily took the next year's Prix de l'Arc de Triomphe, 6 October 1968. Known as 'Weary Willie', the laconic Australian Williamson was a recognised big race specialist whose services were bought by all the top European trainers, including Vaguely Noble's handler, Etienne Pollet.

Gut angelegtes Geld. Vaguely Noble und Bill Williamson gewinnen im nächsten Jahr ungefährdet beim Prix de l'Arc de Triomphe, 6. Oktober 1968. Der lakonische Australier Williamson, bekannt als „müder Willie", war ein anerkannter Spezialist für große Rennen. Der Jockey stand auf der Gehaltsliste aller europäischen Toptrainer, einschließlich Vaguely Nobles Betreuer Etienne Pollet.

Un bon investissement. L'année suivante, Vaguely Noble et Bill Williamson gagnent facilement le Prix de l'Arc de Triomphe, 6 octobre 1968. Mieux connu sous le sobriquet de «Weary Willie» (Willie le pénible), le laconique Australien était reconnu comme spécialiste des plus grandes courses. Les principaux entraîneurs, dont Étienne Pollet, entraîneur de Vaguely Noble cherchaient à l'engager.

Belles of the ball. French owner Madame Suzy Volterra has a broad smile after her filly Belle Sicambre has lifted the Prix de Diane at Chantilly. The horse looks only marginally less amused. Madame Volterra inherited a large string of horses on the death of her impresario husband, Leon, in 1949 and won the Epsom Derby with Phil Drake in 1955.

Ballköniginnen. Die Französin Madame Suzy Volterra freut sich über den Sieg ihres Fohlens Belle Sicambre beim Prix de Diane von Chantilly. Das Pferd scheint kaum weniger zufrieden. Madame Volterra erbte im Jahre 1949 eine ganze Reihe von Pferden aus dem Nachlass ihres Ehemannes und Impresario Leon. 1955 gewann sie das Derby in Epsom mit Phil Drake.

Les belles du bal. Madame Suzy Volterra, la propriétaire française affiche un large sourire après la victoire de sa jument Belle Sicambre dans le Prix de Diane, couru à Chantilly. Le cheval paraît presque tout aussi content. Madame Volterra avait hérité de nombreux chevaux à la mort en 1949 de son mari Léon, impresario de son métier, et remporta même le Derby d'Epsom avec Phil Drake en 1955.

Triomphe triumph.
Mrs Seamus
McGrath gives her
husband's Arc win-
ner Levmoss a
welcoming pat at
Longchamp. A weary
Bill Williamson is in
the saddle, 1969.

Triumph beim
Triomphe.
Mrs. Seamus McGrath
gibt Levmoss einen
anerkennenden Klaps
nach dessen Sieg beim
1969er Grand Prix
de l'Arc de Triomphe
in Longchamp.
Das Pferd stammt
aus dem Besitz ihres
Mannes. Im Sattel
sitzt ein erschöpfter
Bill Williamson.

L'Arc du Triomphe.
Mme Seamus McGrath
donne une tape ami-
cale à Levmoss, le
cheval de son mari
qui vient de gagner
le Prix de l'Arc de
Triomphe à
Longchamp en 1969.
Le jockey Bill
Williamson semble
bien exténué.

'A face like a well-kept grave.' Lester Piggott keeps up with the news at home before riding at Aqueduct race-track, New York, 4 December 1967.

Keine Miene ver-ziehen. Lester Piggott liest die letz-ten Nachrichten aus der Heimat vor seinem Start auf der Aqueduct-Renn-bahn in New York, 4. Dezember 1967.

Impassible. Lester Piggott s'informe des nouvelles de chez lui avant de courir sur l'hippo-drome d'Aqueduct, à New York, 4 décembre 1967.

Death in the afternoon. A mock funeral procession outside the Treasury in Central London, 19 September 1969. Bookmakers were protesting about a new rateable value tax which they feared could put small betting shops out of business.

Der Tod kam am Nachmittag. Ein symbolisches Begräbnis vor dem Londoner Finanzministerium am 19. September 1969. Der Protest von Buchmachern richtete sich gegen eine neue Steuer, die in ihren Augen die Existenz kleiner Wettbüros gefährdete.

Mort dans l'après-midi. Fausse procession mortuaire devant la perception, dans le centre de Londres, 19 septembre 1969. Les bookmakers contestent un nouvel impôt sur la valeur locative imposable, qui pourrait mettre en péril les petits bureaux de paris.

7. A surfeit of excellence
Klasse im Überfluss
Trop de qualités

Breasting the tape. Red Rum, the only horse to win three Grand Nationals (in 1973, 1974 and 1977), makes his acting debut. The equine celebrity, who made countless public appearances in retirement, played the part of a kidnapped racehorse in the television thriller *The Racing Game*, 1979.

Und Action! Red Rum, das einzige Pferd, welches drei Grand Nationals gewinnen konnte (1973, 1974, 1977), gibt sein Debüt als Schauspieler. Der Star des Pferdesports hatte nach Beendigung seiner Rennkarriere zahllose öffentliche Auftritte und spielte 1979 die Rolle eines entführten Rennpferdes im Fernsehkrimi *The Racing Game*.

Sur la ligne d'arrivée. Red Rum, le seul cheval à avoir remporté trois fois le Grand National (en 1973, 1974 et 1977) entre en scène. Le célèbre cheval qui, après sa carrière, a fait de nombreuses apparitions publiques, tint un rôle dans un téléfilm à suspense intitulé *The Racing Game*, tourné en 1979.

The 1970s was unquestionably the Decade of Champions. Red Rum made Aintree his own, lifting three Grand Nationals. Brigadier Gerard and Mill Reef were British colts of the highest class and Vincent O'Brien's Nijinsky carried the flag for Ireland. Allez France and Dahlia, peerless French fillies, showed that the fairer sex could be just as good. The 1975 Arc de Triomphe winner, Star Appeal, proved that Germany was rapidly emerging as a major racing nation. Seattle Slew and Secretariat, who won the 1973 Belmont Stakes by a record margin in record time, ensured that America got in on the act. At Ascot in 1975, Grundy's and Bustino's duel was immediately billed as the race of the century. These were heady days on the Turf and the list of star-studded performances seemed endless. Texan oil magnate, Nelson Bunker Hunt; French art dealer, Daniel Wildenstein; and football pools millionaire, Robert Sangster, all plunged fortunes into the bloodstock markets and raced on an international scale. When Sangster's 1977 Derby winner, The Minstrel, who cost $200,000 as a yearling, was syndicated for $9 million to go to stud in Kentucky, businessmen all over the world began to realise that it was possible to make money out of racing. Things were never quite the same again.

Ohne Frage: Die siebziger Jahre waren das Jahrzehnt der Champions. Red Rum machte sich Aintree untertan und gewann gleich drei Grand Nationals. Brigadier Gerard und Mill Reef waren britische Fohlen höchster Güte, während Vincent O'Briens Nijinsky die Fahne Irlands hochhielt. Die einzigartigen französischen Stutenfohlen Allez France und Dahlia demonstrierten, dass sich das vermeintlich „schwache Geschlecht" hinter den männlichen Artgenossen nicht zu verstecken brauchte. Der Sieg Star Appeals im Grand Prix de l'Arc de Triomphe von 1975 unterstrich die rasche Entwicklung Deutschlands zu einer bedeutenden Pferderenn-Nation. Seattle Slew und Secretariat, der die Belmont Stakes von 1973 in Rekordzeit und mit einem Rekordvorsprung gewann, sicherten den Rang Amerikas im internationalen Pferdesport. Das Kopf-an-Kopf-Rennen zwischen Grundy und Bustino um den Sieg in Ascot 1975 wurde spontan als Jahrhundertrennen eingestuft. Es war eine berauschende Zeit auf dem Turf und die Liste hochklassiger Darbietungen schien beinahe endlos. Der texanische Öl-Magnat Nelson Bunker Hunt, der Kunsthändler Daniel Wildenstein aus Frankreich sowie der Fußballtoto-Millionär Robert Sangster investierten ein Vermögen in den Pferdemarkt und erreichten mit ihren Tieren internationales Niveau. 1977 gewann Sangsters The Minstrel, das als Einjähriges seinen Besitzer 200 000 US-Dollar gekostet hatte, das Derby. Als das Pferd für neun Millionen Dollar an eine Gestütsgemeinschaft aus Kentucky verkauft wurde, dämmerte es Geschäftemachern weltweit, dass mit dem Pferderennen das große Geld zu machen war. Von da an sollte nichts mehr so bleiben, wie es war.

Les années soixante-dix furent incontestablement marquées par de grands champions. Red Rum devint un habitué des victoires à Aintree, en enlevant à trois reprises le Grand National. Brigadier Gerard et Mill Reef, deux poulains de grande classe, représentaient les couleurs britanniques tandis que Nijinsky, le cheval de Vincent O'Brien, défendait celles de l'Irlande. Allez France et Dahlia, des pouliches françaises d'exception, apportèrent la preuve que le sexe dit « faible » n'avait rien à envier à l'autre. La victoire de Star Appeal lors de l'Arc de Triomphe en 1975 démontra que l'Allemagne était en train de devenir un pays important en matière de courses hippiques. Seattle Slew et Secretariat, qui s'adjugeaient le Prix de Belmont avec une avance et dans un temps records, confirmèrent l'entrée en scène des États-Unis. En 1975, à Ascot, Grundy et Bustino se livrèrent un duel sans merci lors d'une épreuve qui fut tout de suite considérée comme la course du siècle. C'était alors l'époque folle du turf et les performances des stars semblaient ne pas connaître de limites. Nelson Bunker Hunt, le magnat du pétrole texan, Daniel Wildenstein, le marchand d'œuvres d'art français ou encore Robert Sangster, le millionnaire américain du loto sportif, investissaient des sommes colossales dans l'achat de pur-sang participant aux courses internationales. En 1977, The Minstrel, le cheval de Sangster, remporta le Derby ; il avait coûté 200 000$ à l'âge d'un an et fut vendu 9 000 000$ à un haras dans le Kentucky, ce qui fit prendre conscience au monde des affaires que les courses pouvaient rapporter gros. Plus rien ne serait jamais comme par le passé.

(Above) Ten out of ten. Trainer Vincent O'Brien leads in Nijinsky and Lester Piggott after the King George VI at Ascot, the Derby winner's tenth successive victory, 25 July 1970. (Opposite) Hobby-horse. Philippe Paquet tells Madame T J Caralli exactly how her Funny Hobby lifted Longchamp's Grand Prix de Paris, 1977.

(Oben) Zehn von zehn. Trainer Vincent O'Brien präsentiert Nijinsky und Lester Piggott nach ihrem Sieg im King George VI. von Ascot am 25. Juli 1970. Es war der zehnte Sieg des Derby-Gewinners in Folge. (Gegenüber) „Mein Pferd ist mein Hobby." Philippe Paquet weiht Madame T. J. Caralli in das Erfolgsgeheimnis ihres Pferdes Funny Hobby ein, mit dem er sich gerade den Grand Prix de Paris in Longchamp geholt hat, 1977.

(Ci-dessus) Dix sur dix. L'entraîneur Vincent O'Brien ramène Nijinsky et Lester Piggott qui vient de signer dix victoires successives dans le Derby, après le Prix du Roi George VI à Ascot, 25 juillet 1970. (Ci-contre) Un hobby passionnant. Philippe Paquet explique à Madame T. J. Caralli comment Funny Hobby a réussi à enlever le Grand Prix de Paris à Longchamp, 1977.

Two pairs. Jump jockeys Richard Pitman (right) and Bill Shoemark and their mounts are caught at the start in December 1972. Ironically, Pitman, who became a BBC racing journalist, was best known for riding a loser, Crisp, who was caught close to home by Red Rum in the 1973 National.

Zwei Paare. Die Hindernis-Jockeys Richard Pitman (rechts) und Bill Shoemark auf ihren Pferden kurz vor dem Start. Der spätere BBC-Pferdesport-Reporter Pitman blieb ironischerweise vor allem wegen einer Niederlage in Erinnerung – bei der Grand National von 1973 wurde er mit Crisp kurz vor dem Ziel von Red Rum noch abgefangen.

Beau doublé. Les jockeys de saut Richard Pitman (à droite) et Bill Shoemark posent au départ de la course avec leurs montures. Ironie du sort : en décembre 1972, Pitman, qui deviendrait commentateur de courses pour la BBC, était surtout connu pour avoir monté Crisp, un cheval qui s'était fait battre sur le fil par Red Rum lors du National de 1973.

Double-header.
Top French trainer
Alec Head and
his jockey son
Freddie attempt to
persuade their Derby
runner Bourbon to
go down to the post,
2 June 1971.

Doppelkopf.
Der französische
Spitzentrainer
Alec Head und
Jockey Freddie,
sein Sohn, ver-
suchen ihr Pferd
Bourbon zum
Start beim Derby
am 2. Juni 1971
zu überreden.

Les grands moyens.
Le célèbre entraî-
neur français Alec
Head et son fils
Freddie, le jockey,
essaient de convain-
cre Bourbon de se
rendre sur la ligne
de départ du Derby,
2 juin 1971.

(Above) Day for night. Runners and riders in Switzerland are photographed through a filter to give the impression of racing at night, 1972. (Opposite) Morning star. The Dikler, the 1973 Cheltenham Gold Cup winner, and Darkie Deacon, a study in concentration in training, 19 February 1970.

(Oben) Den Tag zur Nacht gemacht. Dieses mit einem speziellen Filter aufgenommene Bild von einem Rennen in der Schweiz erweckt den Eindruck, die Veranstaltung hätte bei Nacht stattgefunden, 1972. (Gegenüber) Morgenstern. Diese Nahaufnahme des 1973er Cheltenham-Gold-Cup-Siegers The Dikler mit Darkie Deacon im Sattel zeigt, dass auch beim Training volle Konzentration notwendig ist, 19. Februar 1970.

(Ci-dessus) En négatif. Les chevaux et leurs jockeys sont ici photographiés au travers d'un filtre afin de donner l'impression d'une course nocturne, 1972. (Ci-contre) L'étoile du matin. The Dikler, vainqueur de la Cheltenham Gold Cup en 1973 et Darkie Deacon, font preuve d'une concentration exemplaire à l'entraînement, 19 février 1970.

A vintage crop. (Above) The victorious Mill Reef and Geoff Lewis return after the Derby, 2 June 1971. (Opposite) The brilliant Brigadier Gerard, who was born in the same year as Mill Reef, and Joe Mercer at Ascot before a fifteenth successive win, 24 July 1972.

Eine gute Ernte. (Oben) Die siegreichen Mill Reef und Geoff Lewis nach dem Derby am 2. Juni 1971. (Gegenüber) Das Ausnahmepferd Brigadier Gerard vor seinem 15. Sieg in Folge am 24. Juli 1972 in Ascot. Im Sattel: Joe Mercer. Brigadier Gerard kam im selben Jahr zur Welt wie Mill Reef.

Un bon millésime. (Ci-dessus) Mill Reef et Geoff Lewis, de retour après leur victoire dans le Derby du 2 juin 1971. (Ci-contre) Le brillant Brigadier Gerard, né la même année que Mill Reef, et Joe Mercer à Ascot en route pour une quinzième victoire consécutive à Ascot, le 24 juillet 1972.

Injury time. (Above) Shaken Irish rider Bobby Coonan is supported by two ambulancemen after a heavy National fall, 3 April 1971. (Opposite) Trainer Ian Balding and stable lad John Hallam put on Mill Reef's knee-boots for his first walk since fracturing his left foreleg, 31 October 1972.

Verletzungspausen. (Oben) Zwei Sanitäter stützen den benommenen irischen Jockey Bobby Coonan nach seinem schweren Sturz bei der Grand National am 3. April 1971. (Gegenüber) Trainer Ian Balding und Stalljunge John Hallam legen Mill Reef vor seinem ersten Ausritt nach überstandenem Bruch des linken Vorderbeins Knieschützer an, 31. Oktober 1972.

Des blessures. (Ci-dessus) Choqué, le jockey irlandais Bobby Coonan est soutenu par deux ambulanciers après une mauvaise chute dans le Grand National couru le 3 avril 1971. (Ci-contre) L'entraîneur Ian Balding et le lad John Hallam mettent les genouillères à Mill Reef qui s'apprête à faire ses premiers pas après sa fracture de la patte avant gauche, 31 octobre 1972.

Mudlark. The smile of a delighted, but dirty, Beryl Smith suggests that she cannot wait to get into the saddle again, after riding in Britain's first flat race for women jockeys at Kempton Park, 6 May 1972.

Dreckspatz. Das trotz aller Dreckspritzer zufriedene Lachen von Beryl Smith legt nahe, dass sie es kaum abwarten kann, wieder in den Sattel zu steigen. Die Aufnahme entstand am 6. Mai 1972 in Kempton Park nach dem ersten Flach-rennen für Frauen in Großbritannien.

Un charme certain. Malgré la boue, le visage heureux de Beryl Smith indique clairement son envie de monter de nou-veau au plus vite, après sa participation dans la première course de plat bri-tannique destinée aux femmes jockeys et qui s'est déroulée à Kempton Park, le 6 mai 1972.

French polish. Mexican owner Madame Maria-Felix Berger, exuding glamour, and jockey Yves Saint-Martin admire their French-trained 2,000 Guineas winner Nonoalco at Newmarket, 4 May 1974. Nonoalco, who also took the Prix Jacques Le Marois at Deauville later in the same season, was eventually exported to Japan to stand as a stallion.

Hand angelegt. Die mondäne mexikanische Pferdebesitzerin Madame Maria-Felix Berger und Jockey Yves Saint-Martin sind voller Bewunderung für ihren 2 000-Guineas-Sieger Nonoalco, Newmarket, 4. Mai 1974. Der in Frankreich trainierte Nonoalco, der in derselben Saison auch im Prix Jacques Le Marois in Deauville siegte, wurde später als Deckhengst nach Japan exportiert.

Le chic français. Madame Maria-Felix Berger, la propriétaire mexicaine et glamour, et Yves Saint-Martin admirent Nonoalco qui, entraîné par un Français, vient de remporter le 2 000 Guinées à Newmarket, 4 mai 1974. Nonoalco allait également gagner le Prix Jacques Le Marois à Deauville plus tard dans la même saison et fut finalement exporté au Japon en tant qu'étalon.

Big Red. Secretariat, ridden by Ron Turcotte, wins the Belmont Stakes, the final leg of his US Triple Crown, by a staggering 31 lengths, 9 June 1973. Known as 'Big Red' by legions of fans, the mighty chestnut colt was generally regarded as America's greatest racehorse.

Big Red. Mit unglaublichen 31 Längen Vorsprung gewinnen Secretariat und Ron Turcotte die Belmont Stakes und damit auch die letzte Konkurrenz der amerikanischen Triple Crown, 9. Juni 1973. „Big Red", wie der mächtige Braune von seiner großen Fangemeinde getauft wurde, gilt allgemein als das beste amerikanische Rennpferd aller Zeiten.

Big Red. Secretariat, monté par Ron Turcotte, remporte le Prix de Belmont qui constitue la dernière partie de la Triple Couronne des États-Unis, avec une avance incroyable de 31 longueurs sur le second, 9 juin 1973. Connu de tous les supporters sous le nom de «Big Red», le jeune et puissant alezan était considéré comme le meilleur cheval de course des États-Unis.

Dahlia, owned by Nelson Bunker Hunt, poses after her King George VI win at Ascot, 30 July 1973. The future would not be so bright for Hunt who later had to sell his huge string of horses after unsuccessful speculation in the silver market.

Dahlia, aus dem Besitz von Nelson Bunker Hunt, posiert nach ihrem Sieg im King George VI. von Ascot für die Fotografen, 30. Juli 1973. Später wurde Hunt vom Glück verlassen und war nach erfolglosen Silber-Spekulationen gezwungen, seine Pferde zu verkaufen.

Dahlia, le cheval de Nelson Bunker Hunt pose après sa victoire dans le Prix du Roi George VI à Ascot, 30 juillet 1973. L'avenir allait s'obscurcir pour Hunt qui dut vendre tous ses chevaux de course à la suite de spéculations hasardeuses sur le marché des finances.

Head girl. Another brilliant French filly, Allez France, and Yves Saint-Martin easily take the Prix de l'Arc de Triomphe, October 1974. Allez France, who was owned by Daniel Wildenstein, was prepared by a master trainer of fillies, the colourful Argentinian Angel Penna.

Führendes Mädchen. Allez France, ein weiteres großartiges Füllen aus Frankreich, und Jockey Yves Saint-Martin gewinnen mit Leichtigkeit beim Prix de l'Arc de Triomphe im Oktober 1974. Allez France gehörte Daniel Wildenstein und wurde von dem illustren Argentinier Angel Penna betreut, der ganz auf das Training mit Stutenfohlen spezialisiert war.

Une jument de tête. Encore une brillante jument française, Allez France, montée par Yves Saint-Martin pour s'adjuger le Prix de l'Arc de Triomphe. Allez France, qui appartenait à Daniel Wildenstein, était entraînée par le pittoresque Argentin Angel Penna, spécialiste de la formation des juments.

(Above) Give us a ring. Bill Pyers shows off a diamond ring, his prize for riding Dahlia to victory in the King George VI at Ascot, 30 July 1973. (Opposite) Latest model. Lucky jockey Yasuo Sugawara gets the car, the flowers and the girl, all for winning the Japanese Derby, 28 May 1975.

(Oben) Den Siegern Ringe. Stolz zeigt Bill Pyers den Diamantring, der ihm für seinen Gewinn beim King George VI. in Ascot mit Dahlia verliehen wurde, 30. Juli 1973. (Gegenüber) Das neueste Modell. Der glückliche Jockey Yasuo Sugawara präsentiert seine Siegprämien für den Gewinn des Japanischen Derbys: das Auto, die Blumen, das Mädchen, 28. Mai 1975.

(Ci-dessus) Le prix de la victoire. Bill Pyers montre la bague rehaussée de diamants que lui vaut sa victoire dans le Prix du Roi George VI sur Dahlia à Ascot, le 30 juillet 1973. (Ci-contre) Les tout derniers modèles. Chanceux, le jockey Yasuo Sugawara remporte à la fois la voiture, les fleurs et la fille pour sa victoire dans le Derby japonais, le 28 mai 1975.

Strike action. Striking stable lads, protesting over low wages, try to unseat Willie Carson during a day of disruption at Newmarket's Guineas meeting, 1 May 1975. The 2,000 Guineas, which was late off because of the trouble, was won by the 33/1 outsider Bolkonski, ridden by Frankie Dettori's father, Gianfranco.

Streikmaßnahmen. Wegen zu geringer Löhne streikendes Stallpersonal beim Versuch Willie Carson aus dem Sattel zu heben. Die Szene spielte sich am 1. Mai 1975 während des Guineas-Meetings in Newmarket ab. Die 2000 Guineas, die aufgrund des Streiks mit Verspätung begannen, konnte der 33/1-Außenseiter Bolkonski mit Frankie Dettoris Vater Gianfranco im Sattel gewinnen.

En grève. Les lads en grève protestent contre les bas salaires. Ils essaient de faire descendre Willie Carson lors d'une journée tumultueuse au meeting des Guinées de Newmarket, 1er mai 1975. Le 2000 Guinées, couru à une date ultérieure en raison des troubles, fut remporté par Bolkonski, outsider à 33 contre 1 et monté par le père de Frankie Dettori, Gianfranco.

Sit-in. Stable staff sit down on the Rowley Mile Course at Newmarket in an attempt to stop racing, 1 May 1975. There were angry clashes with spectators who tried to remove the demonstrators. In a bitter aftermath, many of the troublemakers lost their jobs in Newmarket's training yards.

Sit-in. Mit einer Sitzblockade versuchen Stallangestellte den Rennbetrieb auf dem Rowley Mile Course in Newmarket zu verhindern, 1. Mai 1975. Es kam zu Handgreiflichkeiten mit Zuschauern, die die Demonstranten gewaltsam vertreiben wollten. Bitterer Nachgeschmack der Aktion: Viele der Protestierenden verloren anschließend ihren Job beim Trainingscenter von Newmarket.

Sit-in. Le personnel des écuries s'assied sur la piste de la Rowley Smile Course, à Newmarket, afin d'empêcher le départ de la course, 1er mai 1975. Il y eut des heurts violents avec des spectateurs essayant de repousser les manifestants. Plus grave encore : à la suite de ces troubles, nombre de grévistes perdirent leur travail sur les terrains d'entraînement de Newmarket.

Tommy Carberry steers L'Escargot over the final fence ahead of French Tan to win the Cheltenham Gold Cup, at 33/1, March 1970. The same pair won again in 1971, this time at a more sensible 7/2, with Leap Frog in second place.

Tommy Carberry dirigiert L'Escargot über das letzte Hindernis beim Cheltenham Gold Cup im März 1970. In diesem Moment ziehen sie an French Tan vorbei und gehen als 33/1-Sieger ins Ziel. Ein Jahr darauf gewann das Duo erneut, diesmal jedoch vor Leap Frog und bei nur noch 7/2-Wettquoten.

L'Escargot, coté à 33 contre 1 et monté par Tommy Carberry, franchit le dernier obstacle en tête devant French Tan pour remporter finalement la Cheltenham Gold Cup, mars 1970. Ce tandem gagnera de nouveau l'épreuve en 1971 devant Leap Frog, avec une cote de 3,5 contre un.

(Above) The race of the century. The three-year-old Grundy and Pat Eddery (right) win a titanic duel with the year-old Bustino (Joe Mercer up) in the King George VI at Ascot, 1975. Grundy, trained by Peter Walwyn, had won the English and Irish Derby earlier in the season.

(Oben) Das Rennen des Jahrhunderts. Der Dreijährige Grundy und Pat Eddery (rechts) entscheiden das unsterbliche Duell mit dem Einjährigen Bustino (mit Jockey Joe Mercer) im King-George-VI.-Rennen in Ascot von 1975 für sich. In derselben Saison gewann Grundy, trainiert von Peter Walwyn, sowohl das englische als auch das irische Derby.

(Ci-dessus) La course du siècle. Grundy, âgé de trois ans et monté par Pat Eddery (à droite) remporte son duel au sommet face à Bustino, un cheval âgé d'un an et monté par Joe Mercer, lors du prix du Roi George VI, à Ascot, en 1975. Grundy, entraîné par Peter Walwyn, avait déjà gagné le Derby anglais et irlandais, plus tôt dans la saison.

(Above) Style with a smile. A grinning Lester Piggott
(a collector's item, surely?) dismounts from The
Minstrel after victory at Ascot, 23 July 1977.
(Right) Riding-master. One of the maestro's finest
rides. A power-packed Piggott finish propels
The Minstrel to a narrow Derby win in the Queen's
Silver Jubilee year, 1 June 1977.

(Oben) Strahlender Sieger. Der lächelnde Lester
Piggott (ein wahrlich seltener Anblick) beim Absitzen
von The Minstrel nach ihrem Sieg in Ascot am
23. Juli 1977. (Rechts) Rittmeister. Eine der besten
Vorstellungen des Maestros – mit einem kraftvollen
Finish führt Piggott The Minstrel zu einem knappen
Derby-Sieg im Jahre des silbernen Thronjubiläums
der Queen, 1. Juni 1977.

(Ci-dessus) Le style et le sourire. C'est avec le sourire
que l'on voit rarement que Lester Piggott descend de
The Minstrel après sa victoire à Ascot, le 23 juillet 1977.
(À droite) Le maître en action. Une arrivée époustouflante de Lester Piggott propulse The Minstrel vers la
victoire dans un Derby serré, l'année du jubilé d'argent
de la reine, 1er juin 1977.

Rum punch. Jockey Tommy Stack punches the air triumphantly as Red Rum makes racing history by winning his third Grand National at Aintree. This was Red Rum's most impressive National victory. His millions of supporters never had an anxious moment as he beat the runner-up, Churchtown Boy, by an impressive 25 lengths, 1 April 1977.

Rumrennen. Jockey Tommy Stack hebt triumphierend den Arm, wohl wissend, dass Red Rum mit seinem dritten Sieg bei der Grand National in Aintree Renngeschichte schreibt. Dieser Sieg am 1. April 1977 war sicherlich der eindrucksvollste in der Karriere von Red Rum, den seine unzähligen Fans zu keiner Zeit in Gefahr einer Niederlage sahen: Das Pferd schlug seinen Verfolger Churchtown Boy mit beeindruckenden 25 Längen Vorsprung.

Red Rum s'envole. Le jockey Tommy Stack lève triomphalement le bras et Red Rum remporte une course historique en enlevant son troisième Grand National à Aintree, qui reste sa victoire la plus impressionnante dans cette épreuve. Ses supporters n'ont jamais douté un seul instant de sa victoire puisqu'il termine la course avec 25 longueurs d'avance sur son suivant Churchtown Boy, 1er avril 1977.

Rum-runner. Red Rum bares his teeth at a big Haydock Park fence. Brian Fletcher, who rode Red Rum to his first two National wins in 1973 and 1974, is the rider, 8 February 1973.

Rumspringen. Red Rum zeigt einem großen Hindernis in Haydock Park die Zähne, 8. Februar 1973. Im Sattel sitzt Brian Fletcher, mit dem Red Rum seine ersten beiden Grand-National-Siege 1973 und 1974 errang.

Le sourire de la victoire. Red Rum laisse voir sa dentition sur cet obstacle imposant de Haydock Park, 8 février 1973. Il est monté par Brian Fletcher qui était également son cavalier lors de ses deux premières victoires dans le Grand National, en 1973 et en 1974.

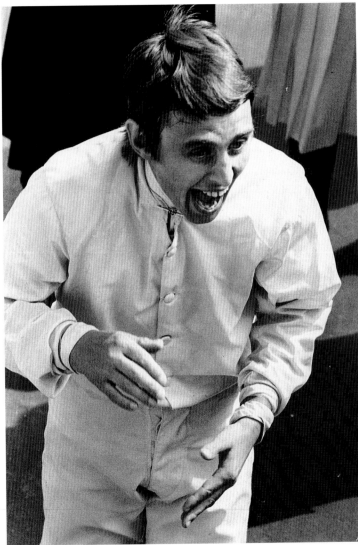

Laughing all the way
to the bank.
Scotland's smallest
export, Willie Carson,
is over the moon
after taking the
200th Derby on
Troy, 6 June 1979.

Ein gut gefülltes
Konto macht immer
fröhlich. Schottlands
kleinster Export
Willie Carson
schwebt nach
seinem Sieg beim
200. Derby auf Troy
im siebten Himmel,
6. Juni 1979.

Un compte bien
garni rend toujours
hilare. Willie Carson,
le plus petit produit
d'exportation écos-
sais, semble au
comble de la félicité
et rit du bon tour
qu'il vient de jouer
en remportant le
200ᵉ Derby sur Troy,
6 juin 1979.

Little and large.
American champion
jockey Willie
Shoemaker and his
wife Cindy at Epsom.
Earlier, Shoemaker,
on Hawaiian Sound,
had finished second
to Shirley Heights
in the Derby,
6 June 1978.

Klein und groß.
Der amerikanische
Champion Willie
Shoemaker mit
seiner Frau Cindy
am 6. Juni 1978 in
Epsom. Kurz zuvor
hatte er mit
Hawaiian Sound das
Derby als Zweiter
hinter Shirley
Heights beendet.

Différence de taille.
Le jockey américain
Willie Shoemaker
et son épouse Cindy
à Epsom. Plus tôt,
Shoemaker, monté
sur Hawaiian Sound,
avait terminé second
du Derby derrière
Shirley Heights,
6 juin 1978.

(Above) Derby starter Alec Marsh on his rostrum, 3 June 1970. (Left) An impressive aerial view of the enormous crowd at Epsom for the 200th Derby in 1979. Note the considerable number of coaches to the left and right of the course; racegoers have traditionally been bussed to the Derby from all parts of the country.

(Oben) Rennrichter Alec Marsh auf seinem Hochstand, 3. Juni 1970. (Links) Eindrucksvoller Blick auf die Publikumsmassen beim 200. Derby von Epsom, 1979. Beachtenswert die zahlreichen Busse rechts und links der Rennbahn, mit denen man traditionell aus allen Landesteilen zum Derby anreist.

(Ci-dessus) Alec Marsh donne le départ du Derby du haut de son estrade, le 3 juin 1970. (À gauche) Une impressionnante vue aérienne de l'immense foule massée à Epsom pour assister au 200ᵉ Derby. À noter le nombre d'autobus à gauche et à droite de la piste. C'est en effet une tradition pour les mateurs de course du pays tout entier que de se rendre au Derby en autobus.

8. Trouble and strife
Vom Regen in die Traufe
Une époque troublée

A marriage made in heaven. Richard Dunwoody on Desert Orchid. The popular grey steeplechaser, who won three King George VI Chases at Kempton Park on the trot and a Cheltenham Gold Cup, thrilled British jumping crowds in the late Eighties.

Eine himmlische Verbindung. Richard Dunwoody auf Desert Orchid. Das populäre Hindernis-Rennpferd gewann dreimal hintereinander bei der King George VI. Chase in Kempton Park und holte sich den Cheltenham Gold Cup. Der Schimmel sorgte in den späten 1980er Jahren beim britischen Publikum für Begeisterung.

Couple divin. Richard Dunwoody sur Desert Orchid. Le spécialiste du steeple-chase à la robe grise, très apprécié du public, a soulevé l'enthousiasme des foules britanniques à la fin des années quatre-vingt en remportant trois fois d'affilée le Prix du Roi George VI à Kempton Park ainsi qu'une Cheltenham Gold Cup.

Arab money may have sent bloodstock prices rocketing through the roof, but racing had more than its share of ups and downs in the Eighties. The taciturn Lester Piggott was sent to prison for tax evasion. Shergar was stolen by IRA terrorists, spirited away from his box on the Aga Khan's Irish stud. When it became clear that the syndicate who owned the stallion was not prepared to pay a ransom, the kidnappers lost their nerve and cruelly slaughtered the horse that had been the easiest Derby winner ever. The decision by many American states in the 1970s to allow horses to race on medication came home to roost. A proliferation of broken blood vessels and lameness among the world's thoroughbreds suggested that some stallions and mares, their defects disguised by legalised drugs in their racing days, were passing on such traits to their progeny. But the dark days were illuminated by rays of sunshine. The American jockey, Steve Cauthen, steered the filly Oh So Sharp to three memorable Classic wins in 1985. Jenny Pitman became the first woman to train a Grand National winner. Like Red Rum, the grey steeplechaser Desert Orchid became a public pin-up. And there were tears of joy when Bob Champion, recently recovered from cancer, won the Grand National on Aldaniti in 1981.

Auch wenn arabische Geldgeber die Preise für Vollblutpferde in die Höhe schnellen ließen, erlebte der Rennsport in den 80er Jahren einige Höhen und Tiefen. Der schweigsame Lester Piggott kam wegen Steuerhinterziehung ins Gefängnis. Shergar wurde von IRA-Terroristen aus seiner Box im irischen Gestüt des Aga Khan entführt. Als klar wurde, dass der Verband, dem der Hengst gehörte, nicht bereit war, ein Lösegeld zu zahlen, verloren die Kidnapper die Nerven und schlachteten das Pferd – den souveränsten Derby-Sieger aller Zeiten – auf grausame Art und Weise. Die von einer Vielzahl amerikanischer Bundesstaaten in den siebziger Jahren getroffene Entscheidung, Pferde, die unter Medikamenten stehen, an Rennen teilnehmen zu lassen, fiel auf die Urheber zurück: Mehr und mehr Vollblutpferde litten unter aufgeplatzten Blutgefäßen und Lahmheit. Diese Tatsache deutete darauf hin, dass einige Hengste und Stuten Gebrechen, die man während ihrer Rennzeit mit legalen Drogen „kuriert" hatte, an ihre Nachkommen weitergaben. Doch es gab auch einige Sonnenstrahlen in diesen dunklen Tagen. Der amerikanische Jockey Steve Cauthen errang mit der jungen

Stute Oh So Sharp im Jahr 1985 drei denkwürdige Siege in klassischen Rennen. Jenny Pitman trainierte als erste Frau einen Grand-National-Sieger. Ähnlich wie Red Rum wurde der Schimmel Desert Orchid als Hindernis-Rennpferd ein gefeierter Star. Tränen der Freude wurden vergossen, als Bob Champion, der erst kürzlich den Krebs besiegt hatte, im Jahr 1981 die Grand National auf Aldaniti gewann.

L'argent massivement investi par les princes arabes fit, bien sûr, exploser les prix des pur-sang, mais cela n'empêcha pas le monde des courses de connaître des fortunes diverses au cours des années quatre-vingt. Le taciturne Lester Piggott fut ainsi emprisonné pour fraude fiscale. Shergar, kidnappé par les terroristes de l'IRA, disparut des haras irlandais de l'Aga Khan. Comprenant que le groupement des propriétaires de l'étalon n'était manifestement pas disposé à payer de rançon, les ravisseurs à bout de nerfs abattirent sans état d'âme le cheval le plus performant du Derby, toutes époques confondues. La décision, prise par de nombreux États américains durant les années soixante-dix, d'autoriser les chevaux à courir tout en étant soumis à un traitement médical, fut lourde de conséquences : de plus en plus de pur-sang dans le monde entier souffrirent de rupture des vaisseaux sanguins ou de claudication, et tout porte à croire que les tares de certains étalons et juments, dissimulées par divers médicaments ingurgités au long de leur carrière, se transmettaient à leur progéniture. Quelques rayons de soleil venaient toutefois éclairer ce sinistre tableau. Ainsi, en 1985, le jockey américain Steve Cauthen, conduisit la jument Oh So Sharp à la victoire dans trois classiques mémorables. Jenny Pitman devint la première femme entraîneur d'un cheval vainqueur du Grand National. À l'instar de Red Rum, Desert Orchid, le spécialiste du steeple-chase à la robe grise, devint la coqueluche du public. Et l'on vit couler des larmes de joie lorsque Bob Champion, tout juste guéri d'un cancer, s'imposa à l'occasion du Grand National d'Aldaniti en 1981.

A tale with an unhappy ending. (Above) Shergar, later to be kidnapped and cruelly killed, takes the Derby by 10 lengths. (Left) Owner the Aga Khan IV leads in Walter Swinburn – known as 'the Choirboy' on account of his cherubic countenance – on the widest margin winner ever, June 1981.

Eine Geschichte ohne Happy End. (Oben) Shergar gewinnt im Juni 1981 das Derby mit dem Rekordvorsprung von zehn Längen. Später wurde das Pferd entführt und grausam umgebracht. (Links) Der vierte Aga Khan, Shergars Besitzer, führt sein Pferd und Jockey Walter Swinburn von der Bahn. Aufgrund seiner engelsgleichen Gemütsruhe wurde Swinburn auch „der Chorknabe" genannt.

Un conte qui finit mal. (Ci-dessus) Shergar, qui devait être par la suite enlevé puis sauvagement abattu, remporte le Derby avec dix longueurs d'avance, juin 1981. (À gauche) L'Aga Khan IV ramène Walter Swinburn plus communément appelé « Choirboy » (jeune choriste) en raison de son visage enfantin après la plus confortable victoire jamais remportée.

(Left) Lester Piggott
after a record-
breaking 28th Classic
win, the St Leger,
on Commanche Run,
16 September 1984.
(Opposite) Bob
Champion and
Aldaniti at trainer
Josh Gifford's
Findon stables after
their National vic-
tory, 6 April 1981.

(Links) Lester Piggott
nach seinem Sieg
beim St. Leger mit
Commanche Run,
16. September 1984,
seinem 28. Erfolg in
einem Klassiker.
(Gegenüber) Bob
Champion und Alda-
niti auf dem Gelände
ihres Trainers Josh
Gifford nach ihrem
Grand-National-Sieg
am 6. April 1981.

(À gauche) Lester
Piggott après le Prix
de St Léger sur
Commanche Run,
16 septembre 1984,
sa 28ᵉ victoire dans
un classique – un
record! (Ci-contre)
Bob Champion et
Aldanati aux écuries
de l'entraîneur Josh
Gifford après leur
victoire dans le
Grand National,
le 6 avril 1981.

Joking jockeys. Champion flat jockey Willie Carson and owner Major-General Sir James D'Avigdor-Goldsmid, splendidly attired in racing tweeds, have a laugh, 1980.

Spaß muss sein. Willie Carson, Jockey-Champion im Flachrennen und der tadellos gekleidete Pferdebesitzer Major-General Sir James D'Avigdor-Goldsmid im feinen Zwirn haben Grund zur Freude, 1980.

Des blagues de jockeys. Échange de plaisanteries entre le champion de plat Willie Carson et le propriétaire de chevaux, le Général de division Sir James D'Avigdor-Goldsmid, vêtu de tweed pour l'occasion, 1980.

Jump jockey Jonjo
O'Neill, who won
two Cheltenham
Gold Cups on
Alverton and Dawn
Run, creases up on
the scales, 1981.

Der Hindernis-Jockey
Jonjo O'Neill, zwei-
facher Cheltenham-
Gold-Cup-Gewinner
mit Alverton und
Dawn Run, findet
die Gewichts-
kontrolle einfach
zum Lachen, 1981.

Le jockey Jonjo
O'Neill, spécialiste
des courses d'obsta-
cles et vainqueur de
deux Cheltenham
Gold Cups sur
Alverton et Dawn,
éclate de rire à la
pesée, 1981.

A study in concentration. (Opposite) Secret Progress's rider slips the reins at a vital stage to ensure a safe landing, 16 April 1980. (Above) John Francome, seven times champion jump jockey but now a television racing presenter, and Don't Touch in perfect harmony, 1984.

Konzentrations-Studien. (Gegenüber) Der Jockey lässt die Zügel locker, um Secret Progress nach einem schwierigen Hindernis die sichere Landung zu ermöglichen, 16. April 1980. (Oben) John Francome, siebenfacher Hindernis-Champion und heutiger TV-Moderator von Pferdesportsendungen, in perfekter Harmonie mit Don't Touch, 1984.

Un modèle de concentration. (Ci-contre) Le cavalier de Secret Progress relâche les rênes au bon moment pour assurer au cheval une bonne réception, 16 avril 1980. (Ci-dessus) John Francome, sept fois champion de saut, devenu aujourd'hui présentateur de courses, est en parfaite harmonie avec le cheval Don't Touch, 1984.

Slipping the field.
The easy winner,
Slip Anchor, and
Steve Cauthen, the
skilful American
rider, are well clear
of the Derby field at
Tattenham Corner,
1985.

Den Verfolgern ent-
wischt. Slip Anchor
und der gewandte
Jockey Steve Cauthen
haben sich in der
Tattenham-Kurve
schon weit genug
vom Feld abgesetzt,
um das 1985er
Derby ungefährdet
zu gewinnen.

Cavalier seul. Slip
Anchor, monté par le
talentueux jockey
américain Steve
Cauthen, remporte
facilement le Derby
en 1985. Il est ici
largement en tête
dans le virage de
Tattenham.

The Kentucky Kid. Steve Cauthen, who was British champion flat jockey three times in the Eighties, attracts the media's attention at Doncaster races, 1987. Cauthen was retained by the Newmarket trainer Henry Cecil, who handled Slip Anchor and the brilliant filly Oh So Sharp, ridden by Cauthen to win a Triple Crown.

Der Junge aus Kentucky. Steve Cauthen, der in den Achtzigern dreimal britischer Flachrenn-Champion wurde, zieht die Aufmerksamkeit der Medien beim 1987er Doncaster Meeting auf sich. Cauthen ritt für den Stall des Trainers Henry Cecil in Newmarket. Cecil betreute Slip Anchor und das fantastische Stutenfohlen Oh So Sharp, mit dem Steve Cauthen die Triple Crown gewann.

Le Kid du Kentucky. Steve Cauthen, trois fois champion de Grande-Bretagne du plat dans les années quatre-vingt, est cerné de journalistes lors des courses de Doncaster, en 1987. Cauthen fut engagé par l'entraîneur de Nexmarket Henry Cecil qui s'occupait de Slip Anchor et de la brillante jument Oh So Sharp. Montée par Cauthen, cette dernière remporta la Triple Couronne.

It never rains in California. A race in progress at the top American racecourse, Santa Anita, Los Angeles, 1988. Elegant palms and the Sierra Madre mountains present a magnificent backdrop to the track which hosted two Breeders' Cup meetings in the Eighties and Nineties.

It never rains in California. Momentaufnahme eines Rennens auf der Rennbahn von Santa Anita, Los Angeles, 1988. Hoch aufragende Palmen und die Berge der Sierra Madre bilden den malerischen Hintergrund für einen der führenden Rennstrecken Amerikas.
In den achtziger und neunziger Jahren wurden hier zwei Breeders' Cup Meetings ausgetragen.

Il ne pleut jamais en Californie. Une course sur le bel hippodrome de Santa Anita, à Los Angeles, 1988. Bordée d'élégants palmiers et offrant une vue magnifique sur les sommets de la Sierra Madre, cette piste accueillit durant les années quatre-vingt et quatre-vigt-dix deux compétitions comptant pour la Breeders' Cup (Coupe des Éleveurs).

Racing down the strand. They're running at Laytown, the unique Irish racecourse where racing takes place on the 3-mile-long golden beach. Local folklore says that a parish priest organised the first meeting on the sands as long ago as 1876.

Strandlauf. Auf der einzigartigen Rennbahn im irischen Laytown führt der Kurs auf einer Länge von drei Meilen über den Strand. Gemäß der lokalen Geschichtsschreibung hat ein Gemeindepfarrer das Rennen auf Sand im Jahre 1876 ins Leben gerufen.

Entre ciel et mer. Course à Laytown, l'hippodrome irlandais où les courses se déroulent sur le merveilleux rivage, long d'environ 5 kilomètres. Selon la légende locale, la première course sur la plage a été organisée en 1876 par le curé de la paroisse.

A step too far. An unfortunate jockey (left) takes the fence before his horse in the Grand National at Aintree. Later, the 28/1 outsider Little Polveir, ridden by Jimmy Frost, provided trainer Toby Balding with a second National winner, April 1989.

Ein Schritt zu weit. Ein Jockey im Pech (links) überspringt das Hindernis bei der Grand National in Aintree vor seinem Pferd. Der spätere Sieg des 28/1-Außenseiters Little Polveir mit Jimmy Frost im Sattel bedeutete den zweiten Grand-National-Erfolg für Trainer Toby Balding, April 1989.

Un pas de trop. Un jockey malheureux (à gauche) franchit l'obstacle avant sa monture lors du Grand National à Aintree. Finalement, c'est l'outsider à 28 contre 1 Polveir, monté par Jimmy Frost, qui permet à l'entraîneur Toby Balding de remporter le Grand National pour la deuxième fois, avril 1989.

Falling from grace. The National is over for an unlucky grey at Becher's Brook first time round, April 1987. The huge ditch is the most difficult fence at Aintree. The fence was named after Captain Becher, who took a dive into the water in 1839. Nowadays, the brook is dry but still lies in wait for the unwary.

In Ungnade gefallen. Für diesen glücklosen Schimmel ist die National bereits in der ersten Runde vorbei. Der große Graben Becher's Brook ist das schwierigste Hindernis von Aintree. Der Graben ist nach Captain Becher benannt, der hier 1839 ins Wasser fiel. Heute ist der Graben zwar trocken, aber immer noch mit äußerster Vorsicht zu genießen.

Tombé des nues. Le Grand National est terminé pour ce cheval gris qui chute au premier passage de la rivière de Becher's, avril 1987. Cet impressionant fossé constitue l'obstacle le plus difficile d'Aintree. Il tient son nom de Captain Becher qui fit un plongeon dans la rivière en 1839. Aujourd'hui, il n'y a plus d'eau dans le fossé mais l'obstacle ne pardonne pas la moindre faute d'inattention.

Leafy Longchamp. The peaceful tree-lined paddock at Longchamp racecourse before the Prix de l'Arc de Triomphe, 1987. Trempolino, trained by France's leading trainer, André Fabre, and ridden by Pat Eddery took France's most valuable race a few minutes later.

Lauschiges Longchamp. Die friedliche baumbestandene Koppel von Longchamp vor dem Start zum 1987er Prix de l'Arc de Triomphe. Kurz darauf feierten Pat Eddery und Trempolino ihren Sieg beim höchstdotierten Rennen Frankreichs. Trempolino wurde von dem französischen Spitzentrainer André Fabre betreut.

Longchamp. Le paddock arboré et paisible de l'hippodrome de Longchamp avant le Prix de l'Arc de Triomphe de 1987. Trempolino, entraîné par André Fabre, le meilleur spécialiste français, et monté par Pat Eddery, remporte ce jour-là la plus prestigieuse des courses françaises.

Searching for the Arc. The Arc field is closely bunched at an early stage of the 1989 race. British raider, Carroll House, and Irish champion rider, Mick Kinane, were the victors and Newmarket trainer Michael Jarvis landed his first Arc.

Alle wollen den Triumph. In der frühen Phase beim Prix de l'Arc de Triomphe von 1989 liegt das Feld noch dicht zusammen. Das britische Jagdpferd Carroll House und der Champion-Jockey Mick Kinane aus Irland holten schließlich für ihren in Newmarket ansässigen Trainer Michael Jarvis den ersten Titel bei diesem Rennen.

En route vers le Triomphe. Les concurrents du Prix de l'Arc de Triomphe de 1989 regroupés en peloton au début de la course. La victoire revint au cheval britannique Carroll House et au jockey irlandais Mick Kinane. Il s'agissait également de la première victoire dans cette épreuve de l'entraîneur de Newmarket Michael Jarvis.

(Above) The world's biggest racehorse owner, Sheikh Mohammed al Maktoum of Dubai at Royal Ascot, 1982. (Right) Arab legion. King Khaled of Saudi Arabia (seated centre) and his entourage watch Derby winning stallion, Mill Reef, parade at Newmarket's National Stud, 11 January 1981.

(Oben) Scheich Mohammed al Maktoum von Dubai, der weltweit größte Rennpferde-Besitzer, in Royal Ascot, 1982. (Rechts) Eine arabische Delegation. König Khaled von Saudi-Arabien (sitzend in der Mitte) und seine Gefolgschaft beobachten den Hengst Mill Reef, Sieger beim Derby, auf dem Gelände des Nationalgestüts von Newmarket, 11. Januar 1981.

(Ci-dessus) Le plus important propriétaire de chevaux au monde, le cheikh Mohammed al Maktoum de l'émirat de Dubai assiste au Royal Ascot, 1982. (À droite) Une délégation arabe. Le roi Khaled d'Arabie Saoudite (assis au centre) et son entourage admirent Mill Reef, l'étalon vainqueur du Derby, aux haras nationaux de Newmarket, 11 janvier 1981.

Victory salute.
American jockey
Angel Cordero
Junior on Open
Mind, the winner
of the Breeders' Cup
Juvenile Fillies at
Churchill Downs,
1988.

Der Gruß des Siegers.
Der amerikanische
Jockey Angel
Cordero Junior und
Open Mind nach
ihrem Sieg beim
Breeders' Cup für
junge Stuten von
1988 in Churchill
Downs.

Le geste de la vic-
toire. Le jockey
américain Angel
Cordero Junior sur
Open Mind rem-
porte la Breeders'
Cup des jeunes
juments à Churchill
Downs en 1988.

Signing on the dotted line. Rider Jonjo O'Neill makes everyone's day, not least an autograph hunter's, after Dawn Run's Cheltenham Gold Cup triumph, March 1986. The Irish mare is the only horse to have won a Gold Cup and a Champion Hurdle.

Bitte unterzeichnen Sie hier. Der irische Jockey Jonjo O'Neill beschert nach seinem Sieg im Cheltenham Gold Cup auf Dawn Run selbst den Autogrammjägern einen großen Tag, März 1986. Die irische Stute ist das einzige Pferd, das sowohl im Gold Cup als auch beim Champion Hurdle siegen konnte.

Une petite signature ? Le cavalier Jonjo O'Neill fait le bohneur de tous et pas seulement des chasseurs d'autographes puisqu'il triomphe dans la Cheltenham Gold Cup avec Dawn Run, mars 1986. La jument irlandaise est la seule à avoir jamais remporté à la fois la Gold Cup et le Champion Hurdle.

Sleeping beauty. The glamour of Royal Ascot has failed to keep this lady racegoer awake on a hot sunny afternoon. Perhaps Bacchus (the god not the horse) had something to do with it, but clearly Gildoran's second successive victory in the Gold Cup has failed to attract her attention, June 1985.

Schlafende Schönheit. Unbeeindruckt vom Rummel beim Royal Ascot gönnt sich diese Rennbesucherin ein Nickerchen in der Nachmittagssonne. Vielleicht lag es an Bacchus (dem Gott, nicht dem Pferd), dass sie Gildorans zweiten Gold-Cup-Sieg in Folge versäumte, Juni 1985.

La Belle au bois dormant. Tout l'éclat du Royal Ascot en cet après-midi ensoleillé n'a pas suffi à tenir éveillée cette dame. Il est possible que Bacchus (le dieu du vin et non le cheval) n'y soit pas totalement étranger. Et visiblement la seconde victoire consécutive de Gildoran dans la Gold Cup n'a pas beaucoup retenu son attention, juin 1985.

Down to earth with a bump. A jump jockey's life can be a dangerous one. Richard Dunwoody and Spring Hay feel the full effects of a bone-crunching fall, 1989. Too many falls and injuries caused the great Irish rider to call it a day ten years later.

Auf dem Boden der Tatsachen. Ein Hindernis-Jockey lebt gefährlich. Richard Dunwoody, der hier mit Spring Hay einen unsanften Abgang macht, kann ein Lied davon singen: Zehn Jahre nach diesem Sturz von 1989 musste der große irische Jockey nach zahlreichen Verletzungen seinen Job an den Nagel hängen.

Un pénible retour sur terre. La vie d'un jockey de steeple-chase est faite de dangers. Richard Dunwoody et Spring Hay en font ici l'expérience avec cette chute spectaculaire, 1989. Dix ans plus tard, l'accumulation des chutes et des blessures devait contraindre le talentueux jockey irlandais à raccrocher.

(Left) After finishing
fourth Princess Anne
talks to trainer
Michael Stoute,
1988. (Opposite)
Prince Charles on
the Queen Mother's
Upton Grey at
Newton Abbot. He
later rode his own
horse, Allibar, to fin-
ish second at Ludlow,
21 May 1981.

(Links) Prinzessin
Anne und Trainer
Michael Stoute nach
einem Rennen, bei
dem sie Vierte wurde,
1988. (Gegenüber)
Prince Charles auf
Upton Grey, einem
Pferd der Königin-
mutter, in Newton
Abbot. Später wurde
er mit seinem
Pferd Allibar
Zweiter in Ludlow,
21. Mai 1981.

(À gauche) La
Princesse Anne
explique à son
entraîneur, Michael
Stoute, pourquoi
elle a terminé que
quatrième, 1988.
(Ci-contre) Prince
Charles sur Upton
Grey, cheval de la
reine mère. Plus tard,
il finira second à
Ludlow sur Allibar,
son propre cheval,
21 mai 1981.

A reason to celebrate. Rhyme 'N' Reason and Brendan Powell take the 1988 Grand National by four lengths from Durham Edition (Chris Grant up). Rhyme 'N' Reason was trained by David Elsworth, whose Whitsbury stable also housed the popular grey, Desert Orchid, at the time.

Rhyme 'N' Reason und Brendan Powell gewinnen die Grand National des Jahres 1988 mit vier Längen Vorsprung vor Durham Edition (mit Chris Grant im Sattel). Rhyme 'N' Reason wurde von David Elsworth trainiert, zu dessen Whitsbury-Stall in dieser Zeit auch der populäre Schimmel Desert Orchid gehörte.

Le triomphe de la raison. Rhyme 'N' Reason, monté par Brendan Powell, remporte le Grand National en 1988 avec quatre longueurs d'avance sur Durham Edition, monté par Chris Grant. Rhyme 'N' Reason était entraîné par David Elsworth, dont les écuries de Whitsbury hébergeaient aussi le célèbre Desert Orchid.

Like father, like son. Trainer David O'Brien's Secreto (left), ridden by Christy Roche, narrowly beats his father Vincent's El Gran Senor in the 1984 Derby.

Wie der Vater, so der Sohn. Christy Roche auf Secreto (links) gewinnt das 1984er Derby knapp vor seinem Vater Vincent mit El Gran Senor. Secreto wurde von David O'Brien trainiert.

Tel père, tel fils. Secreto, le cheval de l'entraîneur David O'Brien (à gauche) monté par Christy Roche, s'impose de peu face au cheval de son père Vincent, El Gran Senor, lors du Derby de 1984.

Straight from the horse's mouth, or whacky races? Two spectators could hardly have chosen more appropriate masks for Kentucky Derby Day at Churchill Downs racetrack, Louisville. Fancy dress and the party atmosphere combine to make a visit to the Kentucky Derby an unforgettable experience.

Pferdeflüsterer. Zum Kentucky Derby Day auf der Rennbahn von Churchill Downs in Louisville hätten diese beiden Zuschauerinnen kaum ein passenderes Kostüm wählen können. Kostümierungen und die Partyatmosphäre machen den Besuch beim Kentucky Derby zum unvergesslichen Erlebnis.

Avez-vous misé sur le bon cheval? Difficile de trouver masques plus appropriés que ceux de ces deux spectateurs du Derby du Kentucky, à Churchill Downs (Louisville). Les déguisements nombreux et l'ambiance de fête contribuent à faire de cette course un événement inoubliable.

'How could my horse have run like that? I really fancied it.' British flat trainer Richard Hannon who regularly saddles 100 winners a season, looks down in the mouth at Newmarket races, 1988. Things had been better at Headquarters the year before, when Hannon won the 2,000 Guineas with Don't Forget Me.

„Wie konnte mein Pferd nur so schlecht laufen? Ich sah es schon als Sieger." Nach einem Misserfolg beim Newmarket Meeting des Jahres 1988 macht der erfolgsverwöhnte britische Flachrenntrainer Richard Hannon ein verkniffenes Gesicht. Im Jahr davor hatte Hannon, der mit seinen Pferden normalerweise 100 Siege pro Saison verbucht, mehr Glück in seinem „Hauptquartier" – damals gewann sein Pferd Don't Forget Me bei den 2 000 Guineas.

« C'est mon cheval qui court comme ça ? Moi qui le voyais gagnant … » 1998. L'entraîneur britannique de plat Richard Hannon, responsable d'une centaine de vainqueurs chaque saison, ne peut réprimer une moue de réprobation à Newmarket. Le sort lui avait été plus favorable l'année précédente, Hannon enlevant le 2 000 Guinées avec Don't Forget Me.

9. Breaking the mould
Auf zu neuen Ufern
La fin d'une époque

Cowboys and Indians. Cherokee Run, ridden by Mike Smith, takes the Breeders' Cup Sprint at Churchill Downs by a hard-fought head from Soviet Problem, 5 November 1994. The North American Breeders' Cup series started in 1984 and has grown to become the richest and most competitive race day in the Turf's annual sporting calendar.

Cowboys und Indianer. Mike Smith und Cherokee Run gewinnen beim hart umkämpften Breeders' Cup Sprint in Churchill Downs mit einer Kopflänge vor Soviet Problem, 5. November 1994. Die nordamerikanische Breeders'-Cup-Serie debütierte im Jahre 1984 und hat sich seither zum bestdotierten und anspruchsvollsten Meeting der amerikanischen Turf-Saison entwickelt.

Cow-boys et Indiens. Cherokee Run, monté par Mike Smith, remporte la Breeders' Cup Sprint à Churchill Downs à l'issue d'une âpre lutte avec Soviet Problem, le 5 novembre 1994. Les épreuves de la Breeders' Cup, disputées aux États-Unis depuis 1984, comptent aujourd'hui parmi les plus relevées et les mieux dotées du calendrier des turfistes.

High-rises. The 1998 Derby winner High-Rise at exercise on the Al Quoz training track in Dubai, 26 March 1999. The skyscrapers of Dubai City form an appropriate backdrop. Al Quoz is the most up-to-date training centre in the world and houses the Maktoum family's best horses during the winter.

Hoch aufragend. High-Rise, Derby-Sieger des Jahres 1998, beim Training auf der Al-Quoz-Übungsbahn in Dubai am 26. März 1999. Im Hintergrund die Wolkenkratzer von Dubai City. Al Quoz gilt als das weltweit modernste Trainingszentrum. Die besten Pferde im Stall der Maktoum-Familie verbringen hier ihre Winter.

Une tour d'ivoire. High-Rise, vainqueur du Derby en 1998, est à l'entraînement sur la piste Al Quoz de Dubaï, prévue à cet effet, 26 mars 1999. À l'arrière-plan se profilent les gratte-ciel de Dubaï City. Al Quoz constitue le centre d'entraînement le plus moderne au monde ; les meilleurs chevaux de la famille Maktoum y passent l'hiver.

Nachmittag. In den USA brach Laffit Pincay Willie Shoemakers Siegesrekord. Die Grenzen des Rennsports lösten sich auf. Das großartige amerikanische Pferd Cigar wurde nach Dubai geschickt, wo es das höchstdotierte Rennen der Welt gewann. Das irische Pferd Vintage Crop reiste nach Australien und holte sich den Melbourne Cup. Hengste wurden vom nördlichen zum südlichen Ende der Welt transportiert, um so viele Stuten wie möglich in einem Jahr zu decken. Einige Pferde laufen immer noch schneller als andere, aber die 1990er haben gezeigt, dass der Sport in den vergangenen 100 Jahren sein Gesicht gänzlich verändert hat.

Durant les années quatre-vingt-dix, l'idée que, somme toute, rien n'était sacré dans le monde des courses finit par s'imposer. Le Derby fut donc disputé le samedi au lieu du traditionnel mercredi. Le Grand National apporta son lot d'événements spectaculaires : en 1993, la course fut annulée à la suite d'un faux départ catastrophique ; en 1997, la crainte d'un attentat à la bombe de l'IRA obligea les organisateurs à évacuer le champ de courses d'Aintree quelques minutes seulement avant le départ. Le Jockey Club, qui gérait les courses britanniques depuis 250 ans, s'effaça au profit du British Horse Racing Board. Des courses d'obstacles furent même organisées durant l'été et les paris sur Internet devinrent monnaie courante. De même, jockeys et entraîneurs n'hésitèrent pas à innover. André Fabre s'occupait de plus de 300 chevaux en France tandis que Martin Pipe, en Grande-Bretagne, entraînait plus de 200 montures gagnantes durant la saison des épreuves de saut. Cheikh Mohammed, le plus gros propriétaire du monde, fit passer l'hiver à tous ses chevaux sous le soleil du désert. À Ascot, Frankie Dettori remportait avec le sourire sept victoires en un seul après-midi. Aux États-Unis, Laffit Pincay effaçait Willie Shoemaker des tablettes des records pour le nombre de courses remportées dans l'ensemble d'une carrière. Les frontières s'estompèrent entre les différents pays. Cigar, le prodigieux cheval américain, fut envoyé à Dubaï, où il remporta la course la plus richement dotée de toutes. De son côté, l'Irlandais Vintage Crop se rendait en Australie pour s'adjuger la Melbourne Cup. Des étalons de l'hémisphère Nord furent envoyés une année dans l'hémisphère Sud pour y saillir de nombreuses juments. Bien sûr, certains chevaux continuaient d'être plus rapides que d'autres mais ces années quatre-vingt-dix annonçaient clairement qu'en un siècle les courses avaient profondément changé de nature.

In the Nineties it seemed that nothing in horse racing was sacred after all. The Derby took place on a Saturday instead of the traditional Wednesday. The Grand National contributed its own fair share of dramatic moments: in 1993 the race was declared void after the débâcle of two false starts; in 1997 an IRA bomb scare caused Aintree to be evacuated minutes before the start of the race. The Jockey Club, which had run British racing for 250 years, handed over control to the British Horse Racing Board. Racing over jumps even started to take place in the summer; betting on the Internet began. Trainers and jockeys broke the mould as well. In France, André Fabre trained four Arc de Triomphe winners. Martin Pipe trained 200 winners in a British jumping season. Sheikh Mohammed, the world's biggest owner, flew his horses out to winter in the desert sunshine. Frankie Dettori exuberantly rode seven winners in one afternoon at Ascot. In the USA, Laffit Pincay broke Willie Shoemaker's record for career wins. Racing's borders became blurred. The great American horse, Cigar, was sent to Dubai where it won the world's richest race. Ireland's Vintage Crop travelled to Australia to steal the Melbourne Cup. Stallions moved from the Northern to the Southern Hemisphere to cover two books of mares in a single year. Some horses still ran faster than others, but racing in the Nineties signalled that the sport had become a very different game over the last hundred years.

In den neunziger Jahren, so schien es, war dem Pferderennsport nichts mehr heilig. Das Derby, das traditionell am Mittwoch stattfand, wurde auf den Samstag verlegt. Die Grand National bot eine ganze Reihe dramatischer Momente. Im Jahr 1993 wurde das Rennen nach zwei katastrophalen Fehlstarts für ungültig erklärt. 1997 wurde Aintree wegen einer Bomben-drohung der IRA wenige Minuten vor dem Start evakuiert. Der Jockey Club, der seit 250 Jahren dem britischen Pferderennsport vorstand, übergab seine Führungsfunktion an das British Horse Racing Board. Hindernisrennen wurden allmählich auch im Sommer ausgetragen. Das Wetten im Internet setzte sich immer mehr durch. Auch Trainer und Jockeys brachen alle Rekorde. André Fabre hat in Frankreich vier Arc-de-Triomphe-Sieger trainiert. Martin Pipe trainierte 200 Sieger einer einzigen britischen Hindernis-Saison. Scheich Mohammed, der größte Pferdebesitzer der Welt, ließ seine Pferde im Sonnenschein der Wüste überwintern. Der übermütige Frankie Dettori ritt in Ascot sieben Sieger an einem einzigen

Tribal gathering. Arab racegoers study the form for the world's richest prize, the Dubai World Cup, at Nad Al Sheba racecourse, 28 March 1999. Although no betting is allowed under Islamic law, Dubai World Cup night, in particular, under a starry Arabian sky, generates plenty of excitement for the locals.

Das arabische Pferdesport-Publikum studiert die Prognosen für den Dubai World Cup auf der Rennbahn von Nad Al Sheba – das Rennen mit dem weltweit höchsten Preisgeld, 28. März 1999. Obwohl das islamische Recht keine Wetten erlaubt, sorgt das Rennen unter sternenklarem Abendhimmel regelmäßig für großes Aufsehen bei den Einheimischen.

Un recueillement religieux. Ces Arabes, amateurs de sport hippique, étudient les pronostics concernant la course la mieux dotée au monde, la Dubaï World Cup, disputée sur l'hippodrome Nad Al Sheba, 28 mars 1999. Si la loi islamique n'autorise pas les paris, la Dubaï World Cup, courue sous le ciel étoilé d'Arabie, est suivie avec passion par les populations locales.

The Italian job.
Frankie Dettori on
Sheikh Mohammed's
Godolphin stable's
Daylami, the winner
of the Breeders' Cup
Turf at Gulfstream
Park, Florida, 1999.

Auf die italienische.
Frankie Dettori mit
Daylami aus dem
Godolphin-Stall von
Scheich Mohammed.
Das Pferd siegte 1999
beim Breeders' Cup
Turf im Gulfstream
Park, Florida.

À l'italienne.
Frankie Dettori
sur Daylami, le
cheval du cheikh
Mohammed, des
écurier Godolphin
remporte la
Breeder's Cup Turf
à Gulfstream Park,
en Floride, 1999.

Delighted Dettori. The charismatic Italian jockey wins the Arc at Longchamp on Lammtarra, 10 October 1995. Lammtarra, who only raced four times in his life, also took the 1995 Epsom Derby. Dettori was Britain's champion jockey in 1994 and 1995.

Siegreicher Dettori. Der charismatische italienische Jockey gewinnt mit Lammtarra beim Grand Prix de l'Arc de Triomphe in Longchamp, 10. Oktober 1995. Lammtarra, der nur vier Mal in seinem Leben startete, siegte auch beim 1995er Derby in Epsom. Dettori wurde 1994 und 1995 britischer Jockey-Champion.

Dettori aux anges. Le charismatique jockey italien enlève le Grand Prix de l'Arc de Triomphe à Longchamp, sur Lammtarra, 10 octobre 1995. Ce cheval, qui n'a couru que quatre fois durant toute sa carrière, a remporté également le Derby d'Epsom en 1995. Dettori a été sacré meilleur jockey britannique en 1994 et en 1995.

High-class Havana. The top American racer Cigar and jockey Jerry Bailey win the inaugural $4 million Dubai World Cup by half a length, 27 March 1996. Cigar was the Horse of the Year twice in the United States and retired with earnings just short of $10 million.

Eine Zigarre höchster Güte. Das amerikanische Top-Rennpferd Cigar und Jockey Jerry Bailey gewinnen das mit vier Millionen US-Dollar dotierte Eröffnungsrennen beim Dubai World Cup am 27. März 1996 mit einer halben Länge Vorsprung. Cigar wurde zweimal zum amerikanischen Pferd des Jahres gekürt und hatte am Ende seiner Karriere Preisgelder in Höhe von insgesamt fast zehn Millionen US-Dollar verdient.

Un havane, s'il vous plaît. Le champion américain Cigar et son jockey Jerry Bailey remportent la première Dubaï World Cup avec une demi-longueur d'avance et s'adjugent le prix de 4 millions de dollars, 27 mars 1996. Élu à deux reprises Cheval de l'Année aux États-Unis, Cigar totalisait près de 10 millions de dollars de gain à la fin de sa carrière.

'It's so beautiful, I don't really want to give it away.' The ruler of Dubai, Sheikh Maktoum al Maktoum, and his younger brother, Sheikh Mohammed al Maktoum, admire the trophy. No worries. Later in the evening, their brother Hamdan al Maktoum's Almutawakel won the Dubai World Cup for the home team, 28 March 1999.

Zu schön, um ihn aus der Hand zu geben. Der Herrscher von Dubai, Scheich Maktoum al Maktoum, und sein jüngerer Bruder Scheich Mohammed al Maktoum bewundern die Trophäe. Aber keine Sorge: Der Pokal blieb in der Familie, denn später am Abend holte ihr Bruder Hamdan al Maktoum auf Almutawakel den Dubai World Cup für das heimische Team, 28. März 1999.

«Au fond, je la garderais bien cette belle coupe». Le maître de Dubaï, le cheikh Maktoum al Maktoum contemple le trophée en compagnie de son jeune frère, le cheikh Mohammed al Maktoum. Vœu exaucé, puisque dans la soirée la Dubaï World Cup allait être remportée par leur frère Hamdan al Maktoum sur Almutawakel, 28 mars 1999.

Misty moment. Two stable lads and their mounts return from early morning exercise at Flemington, the home of Australia's greatest race, the Melbourne Cup, 28 October 1999. A formidable European raiding party was repelled by Rogan Josh, who was trained by Australia's top man, Bart Cummings.

Verschwommene Momente. Zwei Stallburschen beim frühmorgendlichen Training mit ihren Pferden in Flemington, wo mit dem Melbourne Cup das größte australische Rennen stattfindet. Beim Jagdrennen am 28. Oktober 1999 setzte sich Rogan Josh, trainiert vom besten australischen Coach Bart Cummings, gegen die hervorragende europäische Konkurrenz durch.

Un matin brumeux. Deux lads et leur monture reviennent de l'entraînement matinal à Flemington, où se court la plus grande épreuve australienne : la Melbourne Cup, 28 octobre 1999. C'est Rogan Josh, entraîné par le champion australien Bart Cummings, qui parvint à contenir l'armada venue d'Europe.

Foggy interlude. An inmate of the leading American trainer D Wayne Lukas's stable has a welcome wash-down in front of the barn at Churchill Downs, Kentucky, 3 May 1995. Lukas has one of the largest stables in the United States and maintains satellite training barns at many American racetracks.

Zwischenspiel im Nebel. Willkommene Abkühlung für ein Pferd aus dem Rennstall des führenden amerikanischen Trainers D. Wayne Lukas. Im Hintergrund die Stallungen der Rennbahn von Churchill Downs, Kentucky, 3. Mai 1995. Lukas besitzt einen der größten Ställe in den USA und verfügt über Trainingseinrichtungen an vielen amerikanischen Rennbahnen.

Interlude. Un pensionnaire des écuries du meilleur entraîneur américain D. Wayne Lukas reçoit une toilette complète agréable devant l'écurie de Churchill Downs, dans le Kentucky, 3 mai 1995. Lukas possède l'une des plus grandes écuries des États-Unis et de nombreux centres d'entraînement disséminés sur les champs de courses américains.

The pride of Kentucky. The start of the 124th Kentucky Derby, 2 May 1998.
Real Quiet was the winner of the coveted $738,000 prize. Trainer Bob Baffert
also took the race the year before with Silver Charm, ridden by Gary Stevens.

Der Stolz von Kentucky. Start zum 124. Kentucky Derby am 2. Mai 1998. Das
begehrte Preisgeld in Höhe von 738 000 US-Dollar ging an Real Quiet, dessen
Trainer Bob Baffert auch im Vorjahres-Derby siegte, damals mit Silver Charm und
Jockey Gary Stevens.

La fierté du Kentucky. Départ du 124ᵉ Derby du Kentucky, 2 mai 1998. Real Quiet
devait gagner le prix de 738 000 dollars offert au vainqueur. L'année précédente,
l'entraîneur Bob Baffert remporta également la course avec Silver Charm, monté
par Gary Stevens.

The field race away from Churchill Downs' packed stands at a later stage. Unlike in Europe, the pace is always fast and furious in American races.

Kurze Zeit später im selben Rennen. In vollem Galopp zieht das Feld an den voll besetzten Tribünen vorbei. Anders als in Europa wird bei amerikanischen Rennen über die volle Distanz ein enorm hohes Tempo gegangen.

Quelques instants plus tard. Les concurrents s'éloignent des tribunes bondées de Churchill Downs. À la différence des courses européennes, le rythme des courses américaines est toujours effréné.

(Left) Hats off. Real Quiet's rider Kent Desormeaux in high spirits after his Kentucky Derby triumph, 2 May 1998. (Opposite) Unbridled joy. Gary Stevens feels much the same after winning three years earlier on Thunder Gulch, 6 May 1995.

(Links) Hut ab! Real Quiets Jockey Kent Desormeaux lässt den Gefühlen nach seinem Triumph beim Kentucky Derby freien Lauf, 2. Mai 1998. (Gegenüber) Zügellose Freude. Gary Stevens ging es nach seinem Sieg mit Thunder Gulch am 6. Mai 1995 ähnlich.

(À gauche) Chapeau! Le cavalier de Real Quiet, Kent Desormeaux, exulte après sa victoire dans le Derby du Kentucky, le 2 mai 1998. (Ci-contre) Une joie débridée. Trois ans plus tôt, Gary Stevens ressentit une joie similaire après sa victoire sur Thunder Gulch, 6 mai 1995.

Talking through their hats.
Two Australian ladies revel in the carnival atmosphere of Melbourne Cup Day at Flemington racecourse, Victoria, 2 November 1999. A couple of glasses of bubbly and a pair of sparkling smiles appear to suggest that they may have backed some winners.

Mein Hut, der hat…
Zwei ausgelassene Damen genießen sichtlich die Stimmung am Melbourne Cup Day auf der Rennbahn von Flemington, Victoria, 2. November 1999. Die prickelnden Getränke und ihr überschäumendes Lächeln deuten darauf hin, dass die beiden wohl auf das richtige Pferd gesetzt haben.

Dialogue de chapeaux.
Ces deux Australiennes apprécient l'atmosphère de carnaval qui règne le jour de la Melbourne Cup, sur l'hippodrome de Flemington, à Victoria, 2 novembre 1999. Deux verres de mousseux et deux sourires radieux qui laissent supposer que ces deux turfistes ont sans doute misé sur les gagnants.

A fashionable race-
goer seems to be
enjoying herself just
as much at the
Oaks two days later,
4 November 1999.
Is she too close to
the prickly rose
stems for comfort?

Diese modebewusste
Rennbahnbesucherin
hat ebensoviel Spaß
am eigenen Outfit
wie an den Oaks,
die zwei Tage später
stattfanden,
4. November 1999.
Hoffentlich kommt
sie den dornigen
Rosenstielen nicht
zu nahe.

Une turfiste très à
la mode semble
prendre tout autant
de plaisir aux Oaks
deux jours plus tard,
4 novembre 1999.
Mais attention aux
épines.

Take off time. Richard Dunwoody and Amancio combine to take an open ditch at Ascot in immaculate fashion, 5 February 1997. Jump racing did not start at Ascot until April 1965 but the course now stages many important steeplechase and hurdle races during the winter.

Zeit zum Abheben. Mit einem makellosen Sprung nehmen Richard Dunwoody und Amancio diesen Graben in Ascot, 5. Februar 1997. Hindernisrennen werden in Ascot erst seit April 1965 ausgetragen. Inzwischen beherbergt die Rennbahn in den Wintermonaten wichtige Hindernis- und Hürdenrennen.

Le décollage. Richard Dunwoody et Amancio font corps pour franchir impeccablement l'obstacle, à Ascot, 5 février 1997. Aucune course du genre n'était organisée à Ascot avant 1965 mais aujourd'hui, d'importantes épreuves de steeple-chase et de saut de haies s'y déroulent en hiver.

Flying through the air. Choisty and Richard McGrath obtain the necessary momentum to clear the fearsome Becher's Brook in the Grand National. Choisty failed to trouble the winner, Earth Summit, or the placed horses at the finish, 4 April 1998.

Flug durch die Luft. Mit dem richtigen Anlauf gelingt es Choisty und Jockey Richard McGrath am 4. April 1998 das gefürchtete Hindernis Becher's Brook bei der Grand National zu nehmen. Dem späteren Sieger Earth Summit und den Pferden auf den Plätzen konnten die beiden jedoch nicht gefährlich werden.

Le vol. Choisty et Richard McGrath ont suffisamment d'élan pour passer l'impressionnante rivière de Becher's, durant le Grand National, 4 avril 1998. Choisty ne parvint à inquiéter ni le vainqueur Earth Summit, ni les chevaux placés à l'arrivée.

They're for the high jump. Some of the crowd seize the opportunity to jump the famous Aintree fences after the stands are evacuated as the result of an IRA bomb hoax on Saturday 6 April 1997. The National was postponed until the following Monday.

Hochsprung. Nachdem die Tribünen auf Grund einer IRA-Bombendrohung evakuiert wurden, nutzen einige Zuschauer am 6. April 1997 die Gelegenheit, um über die berühmten Hindernisse von Aintree zu springen. Die Grand National wurde auf den folgenden Montag verschoben.

Le grand saut. Certains spectateurs profitent de l'occasion pour sauter les célèbres obstacles d'Aintree après l'évacuation des tribunes consécutive à la fausse alerte de l'IRA, le samedi 6 avril 1997. La course fut reportée au lundi suivant.

A swan out of water. Irish champion jockey Charlie Swan hedges his bets after his mount, Him of Praise, has refused in the Grand National, 4 April 1998. Swan is best known for his partnership with Istrabraq, the winner of three Champion Hurdles in a row.

Wie ein Schwan auf dem Trockenen. Der irische Jockey-Champion Charlie Swan flüchtet sich in die Hecke, nachdem sein Pferd Him of Praise bei der Grand National vor dem Hindernis verweigert hat, 4. April 1998. Besser erging es Swan mit seinem kongenialen vierbeingen Partner Istrabraq, der drei Champion Hurdles in Folge gewann.

Sauvé des eaux. Le champion irlandais Charlie Swan l'a échappé belle après que sa monture, Him of Praise, eut refusé de franchir un obstacle dans le Grand National, 4 avril 1998. Swan est surtout connu pour monter Istrabraq, vainqueur de trois Champion Hurdles d'affilée.

Sprinting for the line. A close finish for a flat race on Sandown Park's straight 5-furlong course, 4 July 1998. The Esher track also stages the British jumping season's last big race, the Whitbread Gold Cup, which has been sponsored by the brewing company for over forty seasons.

Sprint auf den letzten Metern. Ein knappes Finish beim Flachrennen auf dem geraden Kurs von Sandown Park über die Achtelmeile, 4. Juli 1998. Auf der Rennbahn von Esher findet mit dem Whitbread Gold Cup außerdem das letzte große Rennen der Hindernis-Saison statt, das seit über 40 Jahren von der gleichnamigen Brauerei gesponsert wird.

Un sprint vers la ligne d'arrivée. 4 juillet 1998. Arrivée très serrée dans cette course de plat, à Sandown Park sur la ligne droite qui fait plus d'un kilomètre. Sur la piste Esher se déroule également la dernière grande épreuve de saut de la saison, la Whitbread Gold Cup, sponsorisée par une brasserie depuis plus de quarante ans.

Generous in victory. The English Derby winner Generous takes the Irish equivalent at the Curragh, near Dublin, 1991. Alan Munro is the rider of the flashy but brilliant chestnut colt. Trained by Paul Cole at Whatcombe in Berkshire, Generous was owned by Fahd Salman, a member of the Saudi Arabian royal family.

Generöser Sieg. Generous, Gewinner des englischen Derbys, holt sich 1991 auch den irischen Derby-Sieg im Hippodrom von Curragh, nahe Dublin. Alan Munro sitzt im Sattel des ebenso auffälligen wie brillanten braunen Fohlens. Generous wurde von Paul Cole in Whatcombe, Berkshire, trainiert und gehörte Fahd Salman, einem Mitglied der saudi-arabischen Königsfamilie.

Généreux dans la victoire. Generous, vainqueur du Derby anglais, remporte l'équivalent irlandais sur l'hippodrome de Curragh, près de Dublin, 1991. Alan Munro monte le jeune alezan, peu discret mais très brillant. Entraîné par Paul Cole à Whatcombe, dans le Berkshire, Generous appartenait à Fahd Salman, membre de la famille royale d'Arabie Saoudite.

Dirty dancing. The shadows lengthen early on a cold winter's afternoon as the runners take a bend on the all-weather dirt track at Lingfield Park in Surrey, February 1996. Britain has two other all-weather racecourses, at Southwell and Wolverhampton, which also stage flat racing throughout the year.

Dirty Dancing. Die Reiter werfen lange Schatten auf den Lehmboden in einer Kurve der Allwetter-Rennbahn von Lingfield Park, Surrey. Das Bild entstand an einem kalten Winternachmittag im Februar 1996. Neben Lingfield Park gibt es mit Southwell und Wolverhampton zwei weitere Allwetter-Strecken in Großbritannien. Auch dort finden das ganze Jahr über Flachrennen statt.

Une piste poussiéreuse. L'ombre des chevaux s'allonge en ce glacial après-midi d'hiver tandis que les concurrents s'engagent dans un virage de la piste en terre de Lingfield Park (Surrey), praticable en toute saison, février 1996. La Grande-Bretagne dispose de deux autres pistes similaires, l'une à Southwell et l'autre à Wolverhampton, où sont aussi organisées des courses de plat toute l'année.

White mischief. Riders jostle for a good position on the corner during a race on the frozen lake at St Moritz, Switzerland, 3 February 1997. Strangely, horses used to galloping on the turf rarely failed to adapt to racing on the ice.

Weiße Pracht. Positionskampf in der Kurve während eines Rennens auf dem zugefrorenen See von St. Moritz in der Schweiz, 3. Februar 1997. Seltsamerweise kommen Pferde, die den Turf als Untergrund gewohnt sind, meist auch auf Eis gut zurecht.

Le plus malin l'emporte. Les cavaliers cherchent à bien se placer dans le virage lors d'une course sur le lac gelé de Saint-Moritz, en Suisse, 3 février 1997. Curieusement, les chevaux habitués à la pelouse n'éprouvent en général aucune difficulté pour s'adapter à la glace.

Double vision. A huge television screen in the centre of Epsom racecourse gives spectators a magnified view of the Derby action. The horse in fifth position, with the white face, is the eventual winner, Lammtarra, which came in with an unstoppable run, 10 June 1995.

Das Publikum sieht doppelt. Dank eines riesigen Bildschirms im Zentrum des Hippodroms von Epsom entgeht den Zuschauern beim Derby kein Detail. Das Pferd auf Rang fünf (mit der weißen Schnauze) ist der spätere Sieger Lammtarra, der mit einem unwiderstehlichen Lauf ins Ziel ging, 10. Juni 1995.

Double perspective. L'immense écran de télévision situé au centre de l'hippodrome d'Epsom permet aux spectateurs de suivre ce Derby dans les meilleures conditions. Lammtarra, au museau tout blanc, est ici en cinquième position et va remporter la course grâce à un sprint époustouflant, 10 juin 1995.

Screen test. A punter at Sha Tin racecourse in Hong Kong makes an investment in the ultra-modern betting hall, 12 December 1999. There are more bets placed on Hong Kong racing than anywhere else in the world. As betting profits are returned to the sport, the prize money even for run-of-the-mill races is huge.

Test-Bild. Ein Glücksspieler platziert seine Wette im ultramodernen Wettbüro der Sha-Tin-Rennbahn von Hongkong. Beim Pferderennen in Hongkong werden mehr Wetten abgeschlossen als überall sonst auf der Welt. Da die Wetteinsätze in den Sport zurückfließen, werden selbst bei untergeordneten Rennen enorm hohe Preisgelder ausgeschüttet, 12. Dezember 1999.

À la pointe du progrès. Un parieur dépose sa mise dans le centre ultramoderne des paris de l'hippodrome de Sha Tin à Hong-Kong. Hong-Kong détient le record mondial du montant des paris déposés. Les profits étant réinvestis dans les courses, les rapports des épreuves les plus banales sont considérables, 12 décembre 1999.

Focus on France. (Above) The mock Tudor weighing room and unsaddling enclosure at Deauville racecourse in Normandy. (Left) Deauville's modern grandstand, 1 August 1999.

Frankreich im Blickpunkt. (Oben) Der Wiegeraum und der Abreiteplatz der Rennbahn von Deauville in der Normandie sind dem Tudor-Stil nachempfunden. (Links) Die moderne Haupttribüne von Deauville am 1. August 1999.

Vu en France. (Ci-dessus) Le bâtiment de la pesée, en faux style Tudor, et l'enceinte où sont dessellés les chevaux sur l'hippodrome de Deauville, en Normandie. (À gauche) Les nouvelles tribunes de Deauville, 1ᵉʳ août 1999.

Millrace. The famous Longchamp landmark, Le Moulin, towers above the runners as they leave the stalls for the 1995 Prix de l'Arc de Triomphe. Sheikh Saeed Maktoum al Maktoum's Lammtarra beat Freedom Cry by three quarters of a length.

Mühlenrennen. Das Wahrzeichen von Longchamp, die berühmte Mühle, wacht über den Start zum 1995er Prix de l'Arc de Triomphe. Lammtarra, aus dem Besitz von Saeed Maktoum al Maktoum, siegte mit einer Dreiviertel-Länge vor Freedom Cry.

Sur le bief. Les concurrents s'élancent hors des stalles, au pied du célèbre Moulin de Longchamp, pour le départ du Grand Prix de l'Arc de Triomphe 1995. Lammtarra, le cheval de Saeed Maktoum al Maktoum, l'emporte sur Freedom Cry avec trois quarts de longueur d'avance.

What a waste. Her Majesty's Representative at Royal Ascot, the Marquess of Hartington, surveys his fiefdom, 23 July 1999. Hartington is Britain's foremost racing administrator and became the first Chairman of the British Horseracing Board in 1993.

Was für ein Verlust. Der Marquis von Hartington, königlicher Repräsentant beim Royal Ascot, begutachtet seine Gefilde, 23. Juli 1999. Hartington ist der höchste Funktionär des britischen Pferderennsports und wurde 1993 der erste Vorsitzende des neu gegründeten British Horseracing Board.

Quel gâchis! Le Marquis de Hartington, représentant de Sa Majesté au Royal Ascot, contemple son fief, 23 juillet 1999. Hartington, principal responsable des courses en Grande-Bretagne, est le premier président du British Horseracing Board depuis 1993.

It's only champagne.
Frankie Dettori
cracks a bottle of
bubbly after his
1,000th win on
Classic Cliché in
the St Leger at
Doncaster,
9 September 1995.

Es ist nur Cham-
pagner. Frankie
Dettori lässt nach sei-
nem 1 000. Sieg am
9. September 1995
beim St. Leger in
Doncaster auf
Classic Cliché die
Korken knallen.

Ce n'est que du
champagne. Frankie
Dettori fête au
champagne sa mil-
lième victoire en
compétition à l'issue
du Prix de St Leger
qu'il remporte sur
Classic Cliché à
Doncaster,
le 9 septembre 1995.

'We've got to stop meeting like this.' Jerry Bailey gets a passionate embrace after yet another win on Cigar at Arlington, Illinois, 13 July 1996.

„So dürfen wir uns in nicht mehr treffen." Leidenschaftliche Gratulation für Jerry Bailey nach einem weiteren von vielen Siegen mit Cigar in Arlington, Illinois, am 13. Juli 1996.

«On pourrait peut-être se revoir après les courses?» Jerry Bailey reçoit un baiser passionné après sa victoire à Arlington (Illinois) sur Cigar, 13 juillet 1996.

Brown study. A spectator seems to be finding it hard to pick the winners on Gold Cup Day at the Cheltenham Festival, 1992. Not too many punters had the foresight to back the Gold Cup winner, Cool Ground, who started at 25/1.

Brotlose Studien. Dieser Zuschauer hat augenscheinlich Schwierigkeiten, seine Favoriten am Gold Cup Day im Rahmen des 1992er Cheltenham Festivals zu bestimmen. Die wenigsten Wettfreunde hatten auf den späteren Sieger Cool Ground gesetzt, der mit 25/1 ins Rennen ging.

En pleine réflexion. Ce spectateur semble douter de l'issue de la Gold Cup, courue lors du Festival de Cheltenham, 1992. De fait, peu de parieurs avaient prévu la victoire de Cool Ground, coté à 25 contre 1 au départ de la course.

Viewing from a distance. Jumping trainer David Nicholson concentrates on his Cheltenham runner, 12 November 1999. Nicholson, formerly a top jockey, was brought up at his father Frenchie's stables next to the course.

Fernstudien. Der Hindernis-Trainer David Nicholson hat sein Pferd auf der Cheltenham-Rennbahn fest im Visier, 12. November 1999. Nicholson, früher selbst Spitzenjockey, wuchs im Umfeld der Stallungen seines Vaters Frenchie auf, in unmittelbarer Nähe der Rennbahn.

Avec du recul. L'entraîneur David Nicholson suit la course de son cheval à Cheltenham, 12 novembre 1999. Nicholson a grandi non loin des écuries Frenchie de son père, près de l'hippodrome et réalisa une brillante carrière de jockey.

Making a stand.
Record-breaking
jump jockey
Tony McCoy in
celebratory mood
after taking the
Champion Hurdle
at Cheltenham on
Make A Stand,
11 March 1997.

Stehende Ovation.
Der Rekordhalter
im Hindernisrennen,
Tony McCoy, ist in
Feierstimmung,
nachdem er auf
Make A Stand beim
Champion Hurdle
in Cheltenham
gewinnen konnte,
11. März 1997.

Bonheur partagé.
Tony McCoy, le
jockey de saut,
détenteur de records
absolus, laisse éclater
sa joie après sa
victoire dans le
Champion Hurdle
à Cheltenham, sur
Make a Stand,
11 mars 1997.

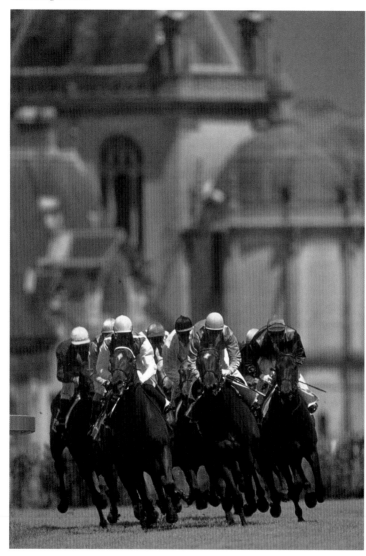

The runners race past the famous chateau at Chantilly, France's most picturesque racecourse, 6 June 1999. Chantilly is also home to many French training stables and has fantastic working grounds in the forest.

Das Feld passiert das berühmte Chateau von Chantilly, dem wohl malerischsten Hippodrom Frankreichs, 6. Juni 1999. Chantilly beherbergt mehrere französische Trainingszentren und ist bekannt für exzellente Bodenverhältnisse in den Waldgebieten, die ein optimales Training ermöglichen.

Peloton de course devant le célèbre château de Chantilly, doté de l'hippodrome français le plus pittoresque, 6 juin 1999. L'hippodrome, où de nombreux entraîneurs français ont installé leurs écuries, dispose en outre de magnifiques terrains d'entraînement dans la forêt.

Bottoms up. Action during the Chester Cup, 7 May 1997. Chester is Britain's oldest track. In addition to substantial prize money, owners of Chester Cup winners always receive the added bonus of a massive Cheshire cheese. Racing first took place on the Roodeye in the 16th century.

Rück-Sicht. Eine Momentaufnahme vom Chester Cup am 7. Mai 1997. Chester ist die älteste Pferderennbahn Großbritanniens; das erste Rennen fand hier im 16. Jahrhundert statt. Neben einem beachtlichen Preisgeld erhalten die Eigentümer der Chester-Cup-Sieger jedes Mal einen großen Cheshire-Käse.

Plus haut! Des coureurs en pleine action durant la Chester Cup, 7 mai 1997. La piste de Chester est la plus ancienne de Grande-Bretagne. La course est dotée d'une prime financière importante et les vainqueurs se voient en outre remettre un énorme fromage du Cheshire. Les premières courses y furent organisées sur le Roodeye dès le XVIe siècle.

Pleased as Punch. Top French jockey Olivier Peslier and Peintre Célèbre after winning the Arc, 5 October 1995. Peintre Célèbre was one of the easiest Arc winners ever, but never ran again, due to a leg injury.

Stolz wie Oskar. Der französische Top-Jockey Olivier Peslier und Peintre Célèbre nach ihrem Sieg beim Prix de l'Arc de Triomphe, 5. Oktober 1995. Peintre Célèbre gehörte zu den souveränsten Siegern aller Zeiten, konnte allerdings auf Grund einer Beinverletzung nie wieder laufen.

Heureux comme un roi. Olivier Peslier, le champion français, vient de remporter le Prix de l'Arc de Triomphe sur Peintre Célèbre, 5 octobre 1995. Ce dernier enleva la course avec une facilité rarement vue jusqu'alors mais ne courut plus jamais, en raison d'une blessure à la patte.

Whiplash. British champion jockey Kieren Fallon asks Great Dane to step on the gas to score at Goodwood, 20 May 1999. Despite being sacked by Henry Cecil for alleged impropriety in July 1999, the volatile Irishman still managed to retain his title.

Nach vorne gepeitscht. Der britische Jockey-Champion Kieren Fallon versucht Great Dane Beine zu machen, um in Goodwood zu punkten, 20. Mai 1999. Obwohl er von Henry Cecil im Juli 1999 wegen angeblicher Unfähigkeit entlassen wurde, behielt der launische Ire seinen Champion-Titel.

À coups de trique. Le champion britannique Kieren Fallon veut forcer l'allure de Great Dane pour remporter la course à Goodwood, 20 mai 1999. L'Irlandais volant fut licencié par Henry Cecil en juillet 1999 pour mauvaise conduite mais parvint à conserver son titre.

Your number's up. Veteran jockey Laffit Pincay Junior beats Willie
Shoemaker's incredible total of career wins at Hollywood Park,
Los Angeles. Irish Nip is his willing partner for a mind-boggling number
of 8,834 victories.

Magische Zahl. Der Jockey-Altmeister Laffit Pincay Junior bricht
Willie Shoemakers Rekordmarke und fährt den sage und schreibe
8 834. Sieg seiner Karriere ein. Sein Erfüllungsgehilfe im Hollywood
Park von Los Angeles ist Irish Nip.

Un record étourdissant. Le jockey vétéran Laffit Pincay améliore l'ancien
record de victoires de Willie Shoemaker à Hollywood Park (Los Angeles).
Il monte ici Irish Nip, avec lequel il signe une époustouflante 8 834ᵉ victoire.

(Above) Safety in numbers. Pincay gets a piggyback through the crowd after equalling 'the Shoe's' record on I Be Casual two races earlier, 9 December 1999. The popular rider won the Belmont Stakes three years in a row for trainer Woody Stephens in the 1980s. (Following spread) Darkest day. Storm clouds threaten the competitors in the 1994 Derby.

(Oben) Ausgleich. Zwei Rennen zuvor konnte Pincay auf I Be Casual den Rekord von „The Shoe" egalisieren und wird auf Schultern durch die Menge getragen, 9. Dezember 1999. Der populäre Jockey gewann unter Trainer Woody Stephens in den achtziger Jahren drei Mal in Folge bei den Belmont Stakes. (Folgende Doppelseite) Drohende Wolken hängen über den Teilnehmern beim Derby von 1994.

(Ci-dessus) Des chiffres éloquents. Pincay est porté en triomphe par la foule après avoir égalisé le record de « Shoe » sur I Be Casual, 9 décembre 1999. Le populaire jockey remporta trois fois de suite le Prix de Belmont dans les années quatre-vingt, avec l'entraîneur Woody Stephens. (Pages suivantes) Une sombre journée. La tempête menace les concurrents du Derby en 1994.

Index

About the pictures in this book

This book was created by The Hulton Getty Picture Collection which comprises over 300 separate collections and 18 million images. It is a part of Getty Images Inc., with over 70 million images and 30,000 hours of film. Picture sources for this book include: **Hulton Getty and Allsport**. Both are part of Getty's press and editorial sales channel **www.gettysource.com**

How to buy or license a picture from this book

All non-Hulton images are credited individually below.

Picture licensing information

For information about licensing any image in this book, please phone **+ 44 (0)20 7579 5731,** fax: **44 (0)20 7266 3154** or e-mail **chris.barwick@getty-images.com**

Online access

For information about Getty Images and for access to individual collections go to **www.hultongetty.com.** Go to **www.gettyone.com** for creative and conceptually oriented imagery and **www.gettysource.com** for editorial images.

Buying a print

For details on how to purchase exhibition quality prints call The Hulton Getty Picture Gallery, phone **+ 44 (0)20 7276 4525** or e-mail **hulton.gallery@getty-images.com**

Acknowledgements

Allsport:

Allsport 321, 326, 343-345, 348-349, 370
Broekema, Tim 384
Bruty, Simon 363
Cannon, David 335
Cole, Chris 338, 340, 375, 383, 385
Cole, Phil 359-360, 378, 381, 390
Frakes, Bill 350
Grayson, Steve 392-393
Herbert, Julian 356-357, 361, 374, 379-380, 382, 386-389, 391
Hewitt, Mike 373
Kinnaird, Ross 371
Lyons, Andy 358, 364, 367
Martin, Bob 336-337
Milligan, Stuart 362, 368-369
Pensinger, Doug 353
Powell, Mike 332, 334
Rogers, David 372

Rondeau, Pascal 325, 351
Smith, Dan 333, 339
Squire, Jamie 365-366
Stewart, Rick 342
Want, Anton 376-377

Band, Alan 295
Gallagher, Rob 394-395
Observer, The 328-329, 331, 346
Smith, Chris 292